Praise for
What Do You Want to Create Today?

"An inspiring, 'inside-out' view of building a life that works. Tobin has an engaging, informal way of writing, making it more likely you will absorb and use his ideas. Practical ideas illustrated through stories of success, failure, and everything in between. Learn from his experience."

—Geoff Bellman, consultant and bestselling author of *Extraordinary Groups* and *Consultant's Calling*

"Anyone in business or going into business should ask the question 'Do I have the courage to be happy and successful?' If you are not sure of your answer, read this book."

—Jim Alley, Senior Vice President (Retired) at Mattel, Inc.

"Bob Tobin is an expert on how to turn around an organization, a team, or a life. In his book, *What Do You Want to Create Today?*, he shares his potent wisdom for adding meaning and passionate productivity to your workplace."

—Mark Levy, founder of Levy Innovation and author of *Accidental Genius: Using Writing to Generate Your Best Ideas, Insight, and Content*

"Bob Tobin's essential new book gets at the heart of today's professional challenge: a choice between following the 'safe' path, which is getting less secure every day, and finding the courage to create a unique and amazing life. Mixing professional insights with engaging personal anecdotes, Tobin has provided a smart and practical guide for anyone who wants to get inspired and take action."

—Dorie Clark, author of *Reinventing You* and HBR/Forbes contributor

"Bob is an inspiration. This wonderful book will help you succeed and have fun in work—and more importantly—in life!"

—Garr Reynolds, bestselling author of *Presentation Zen* and *The Naked Presenter*

"Bob Tobin's approach to career satisfaction starts with the most important element: YOU. He throws away the simplistic formulas for success that bind you into prescribed career paths and instead shows you how to achieve your true ambitions by tapping into your individual creativity. This is an important book for anyone wondering why they are not happy at work and what they can do to change that."

—Melanie Billings-Yun, PhD, author of *Beyond Dealmaking*

"Most of us at some time dream of doing what we really want, but are locked in our current reality. This book is almost a 'how to' manual for believing in oneself. Bob Tobin shares his experience from the beginning, as a successful consultant and educator who felt something missing. Bob allows us to share his thoughts and feelings in a way that encourages the reader to examine their own situation. Bob Tobin is a living example of what is possible if one has the faith and courage to take that first step toward being truly happy."

—Kiku Taura, Former Head of Human Resources at UBS Global Asset Management

What Do You Want to Create Today?

What Do You Want to Create Today?

Build the Life You Want at Work

DR. BOB TOBIN

BenBella Books, Inc.
Dallas, TX

BenBella Books, Inc.
10300 N. Central Expressway
Suite #530
Dallas, TX 75231
www.benbellabooks.com
Send feedback to feedback@benbellabooks.com

Printed in China
10 9 8 7 6 5 4 3 2 1

Library of Congress Cataloging-in-Publication Data
Tobin, Bob.
  What do you want to create today?: build the life you want at work /
Dr. Bob Tobin.
    pages cm
  Includes bibliographical references and index.
  ISBN 978-1-940363-15-8 (trade cloth: alk. paper) — ISBN 978-1-940363-57-8 (electronic) 1. Success. 2. Personality. 3. Conduct of life. I. Title.
  BF637.S8T63 2014
  650.1—dc23

                                                                  2014005355

Editing by Brian Nicol
Copyediting by Stacia Seaman
Proofreading by Jenny Bridges and
    Michael Fedison
Cover design by Sarah
    Dombrowsky

Text design by Publishers' Design
    and Production Services, Inc.
Text composition by Integra
    Software Services Pvt. Ltd,
Printed by Guangzhou Yicai Printing
    Co. Ltd through Four Colour
    Print Group

Distributed by Perseus Distribution
www.perseusdistribution.com

To place orders through Perseus Distribution:
Tel: (800) 343-4499
Fax: (800) 351-5073
E-mail: orderentry@perseusbooks.com

Significant discounts for bulk sales are available. Please contact
Glenn Yeffeth at glenn@benbellabooks.com or (214) 750-3628.

To Hitoshi

Contents

Introduction

I f there had been a contest twenty-five years ago for the person least likely to write a book like this, I would have been the winner, hands down. No questions asked. I was someone with a good education and experience as a professor and a consultant with a good salary, recognition, and prestige.

The only problem was that work just did not work for me. I was good at my job, but I didn't feel like I was being as successful as I could be. Truthfully, I was having a lot of trouble at work. I was unhappy and unsatisfied. You might even say miserable some days. And I couldn't figure out what to do, although I tried.

When I took what I thought would be a temporary assignment in Asia, I had a chance to make a fresh start and I made up my mind that things would be different. It was either now or never for me. I asked myself a lot of questions. I kept a journal; I paid attention to what others said; I kept on pushing myself outside my comfort zone; I listened to my students, clients, and colleagues; and I began to figure things out for myself.

It took me a while, but I learned and developed an approach to working that allowed me to have the kind of life at work I had only dreamed of before. I became much happier and more satisfied at work. And as I was figuring out things for myself, I began to contribute more of what I knew to others.

I was able to create a life at work that not only worked for me, but one that other people told me they wanted as well. I wasn't always sure whether what I knew was something I could explain. There were times when I couldn't identify specifically what it was I had learned or what I was doing.

But as other people took notice, they wanted to know more. They'd tell me I was a great role model for them. When I first heard this, I couldn't believe it. I, who struggled so much before and took a long time to figure things out? They'd see me at work or at social occasions and would ask me, "How do you do it?" Initially, I didn't know what they meant. What was *it*? How could I explain what I knew to them?

Several years ago I told myself I had to figure out exactly what I was doing. I got tired of not being able to answer people's questions about my approach. Even more than that, I wanted to help others have a similar satisfying work experience. I began to analyze more of what I did in order to answer the questions I kept getting from others.

I made a project out of studying my own behavior, actions, and thinking. I thought deeply about what I was doing. I started writing down more about what I did and how I did it.

I began to speak at conferences throughout the United States and Asia about the important elements in my approach. I shared what I knew with my students and clients. This book, *What Do You Want to Create*

Today?, is the result of those years I spent identifying, developing, and teaching this approach to others.

If you want your life at work to be better, I'm sure this book will help. It's an approach you too can learn. You will learn to work with purpose, passion, and power. That's why I wrote this book.

So now it's your turn. The approach and the experiences I detail will enable you to build the life you want at work, a life you may never have thought possible. Many of those experiences are my own, of course; others are those of friends and clients, several of whom requested I change their names to preserve their anonymity.

But before we get into all of that, allow me to share a bit of my backstory and a few more details about how it all started.

CHAPTER ONE

How It All Started

What makes people successful? How can *I* be successful? How can I build the kind of life I want at work? How can I use more of what I know? How can I grow more fully as a person through my work? These are the questions that have interested me all my life. They may have interested you as well.

I got a lot of advice from my parents, friends, and teachers about how to succeed and what career path to follow, but there was only one problem: None of it seemed right. None of it seemed to fit me. My uncle recommended I start my career selling a line of women's clothes, but that was the last thing I wanted to do. My university teachers told me to "be a CPA" or "start in sales and then move into marketing." Marketing might have worked, but I hated accounting and flunked it the first time I took it. I knew I would have to follow my own path, but I was not sure how. I wanted to develop a way of working that would be mine alone, but I struggled to figure out how to do it. I spent a lot of time trying to fit in.

As a student at the University of Massachusetts in Amherst in the late 1960s, one of my favorite activities was looking through the thick college course catalog and studying the background and degrees of my professors. I memorized the courses they taught, their educational backgrounds, and the names of the schools where they had worked before.

One professor had only a master's of science but he was the associate head of the chemistry department, which had many PhDs. Why was he the associate head, I wondered, and how could he supervise so many Ivy League PhDs? And why was the longtime assistant head of the news office, who had a master's, reporting to someone much younger who was just hired and had only a bachelor's?

I knew I should have been studying, but that catalog fascinated me. I even had a few compatriots with the same obsession. The guys across the hall from me in the dorm would do battle with me to see who knew the most about the professors. They didn't even have to be our professors, just any professor in the university. "Where did Robert D. Thompson get his PhD?" one of us would shout out. Someone would answer, "University of Texas." "Correct," another would reply.

"Where did Ken Stevens get his BA?" "Princeton." "Right." "Name two government professors who got their PhDs at Columbia." It went on like this for hours.

I was surprised when I later became a professor and found out that most students don't really pay attention to such things. I've never met a student who played this game with their friends. But for me, it was fun. I was curious about careers and what made people successful.

It became clear to me as a university student that people who attained a certain status needed more than education, experience, or even a particular set of skills. There was something else. Was it luck? Was it a particular personality trait that made people stand out? I didn't know the answers, but I wanted to find them. That became a big part of my life's work.

How about you? What are your theories about why some people become successful? How did you come up with these theories?

When I was growing up, I listened to my father come home every night and talk about work. He owned a drugstore that provided our family with a middle-class standard of living. Every night, he'd come home and rehash the day's problems, focusing on what happened with his employees and customers. He'd talk about how he wanted to fire one of the pharmacists or clerks. He'd rail against customers who didn't pay on time. He'd be angry about the police who would come in for freebies. This was a nonstop nightly saga and I just listened. Work sounded like hell. It was not something I was looking forward to, but I also wondered why work had to be filled with so much angst.

I am sure now that listening to my father set me on my path to discover and develop a different way of working. I didn't think work should be painful.

I spent a lot of my time as a student, consultant, and professor considering how to have a career focused on achievement, satisfaction, reaching my potential, and using more of my talents. Eventually, I did find my way, after many ups and downs. I could have used a book like this when I started out.

When I graduated from college, I vowed to work in a very different way than my father, but it didn't turn out to be that easy. I didn't know where to start or what to do. And there were many people in the places I worked who said I should do what I was told and follow the pack. Besides, there were bills to pay, projects to complete, deadlines, peer pressure, bosses, clients and coworkers to deal with, and things I wanted to buy.

As I look back now, the biggest obstacle was really my lack of knowledge about *how* to work. I didn't know any other way except the way I saw other people work. And I lacked the confidence to pursue my own path.

In one of my first jobs out of college, I started as a researcher in a consulting firm and eventually moved into a role doing curriculum development, training, and consulting. The clients were most often large organizations. I was in my twenties and working with executives and government officials. I was able to observe the way they worked.

As a young consultant, I got the project work done, but it was always the people that interested me most: how they worked, how they got along with others, their life outside of work, how they led their organizations, the career paths they were on. Consulting gave me a chance to observe the clients up close over a long period of time, as some of the projects continued for several years. Consulting permitted me to indulge my curiosity.

The consulting projects might have been challenging and interesting, but I wasn't satisfied with my own work situation. I often put in seventeen hours a day, six or seven days a week; I had little time for anything else. I didn't have much of a social life. The only parties I went to were work parties or events with clients. I lived on sandwiches and take-out food. My only exercise was walking from my office to the coffee machine. Before long I was smoking three packs of Marlboros a day to relieve the stress. There had to be a better way than this. I was definitely on the wrong track.

While still working as a consultant, I began a doctoral program in human and organizational development at Boston University. I wanted to learn everything I could about motivation, quality of life, psychology, sociology, leadership, organizations, and communication. I took an overload of courses and studied with the best professors I could find. I had a tremendous desire to learn and eventually share what I knew with others as a professor and consultant. But there was clearly another reason for going to graduate school, which I recognize now: I needed to make my own life better.

After I finished my doctorate, I moved to Southern California, began my career as a professor, and also did management training for big companies. I stuck to the conventional formula and put out the same message as other professors and consultants. I taught students and conducted management training courses ripped straight out of the pages of textbooks. I lectured on the functions of leadership, theories of motivation, and the obstacles to organizational communication At the university, I got promoted to associate professor within a year and was even selected professor of the year by students.

I delivered the content with passion and got good feedback from the students and the training clients, but it wasn't enough. I was just following the pack. I also was not prepared for the minefield of faculty politics and the university bureaucracy.

As I gained more self-knowledge, experience, and confidence, I began to teach more of what I knew. I taught what was not in the books. I forged strong relationships with the students, but it was tough for me to get along with the other faculty members. I was the first new faculty member in almost ten years, one of the few with a doctorate, and it was no place for innovation. When it came time for my tenure vote, I was denied and had to leave the university.

Not being granted tenure was a tough blow, but I realize now it was truly a lucky break. Eventually, I had time to rethink how I worked and look for a place that would value me and allow me to work in a way that was true to me.

There are those times when getting fired or leaving a certain job propels you to do something better. This was one of those times.

I vowed to pay more attention to understanding a situation before taking action, and I focused on developing stronger relationships with colleagues at work. I spent another year in Southern California consulting for large companies and government agencies, and I taught in the undergraduate and MBA programs at Pepperdine University. I taught more of what I was learning about life and work from my own experience—not just from the manual and text—and was beginning to have the kind of work life I wanted.

I never thought I would leave Southern California, but a friend told me about a position with Chapman University, which changed the direction of my life and helped me put everything I knew into action. Chapman hired me for a project with the U.S. military in Asia, helping military personnel transition into civilian jobs. I taught in the university's graduate programs and counseled military officers and government workers in planning their careers after they left government service.

Every two months, I went to a different military base and often to a different country. I'd start up the project and help people plan the transitions they'd be making as the military downsized. I traveled to bases in Korea, Guam, the Philippines, and Japan.

Instead of coming across as an expert, I tried to understand the military culture. I focused on what the participants needed and shared my own experiences with them. I could understand what they were going through, since I was going through my own transition as I went from base to base. I had never been in the military or in Asia before, so I spent time learning about the military life and local cultures in order to add the most value to my teaching.

I appreciated more of my own skills. I didn't try to blend in or be like everyone else, nor did the military expect me to conform. The program participants knew I was a civilian and wanted me to contribute my unique knowledge. Military culture actually has more freedom than some companies and universities I have worked with. It's a place where you can find a niche as long as you are adding value.

Most of the other project instructors lectured from textbooks, parroting the usual formulas for success on the "outside." They taught participants about the human resource management cycle, the six steps of job hunting, and the roles and functions of leadership. But they didn't *connect* with the people in the program.

My approach to teaching and consulting was more "inside-out" than "outside-in." I focused on helping participants understand themselves and strengthen their courage, creativity, and confidence. My motto was *Every day fresh*. This is how I was beginning to live and how I encouraged them to live.

Work for me was becoming more of what I had always wanted it to be. I liked the discussions in the classrooms. I was learning as I taught. I began to develop a much richer life outside of work as well. Many of the military personnel invited me to their homes for dinners, barbecues, and holiday celebrations. I rekindled my interest in art, which had been dormant for so many years. I had planned on staying overseas for only a year, but I signed up for another year. Finally, work was working out well. And there were even better times to come.

Toward the end of my second year on the military project, I decided to stay in Japan instead of returning to California. I gave notice and left my job with the military. I thought I would eventually go back to live and work in America, but Japan seemed to be the perfect place for me to use what I knew and for what I had to learn. It was the early '90s, the time of the economic bubble in Japan, and there were consulting opportunities helping Japanese companies expand overseas. As someone who loves art and design, I appreciated the minimalist aesthetic that I found in Japan. I also was attracted to the focus on groups and teamwork and the lack of overt conflict. I knew I had to learn how to function as a member of a group and learn about harmony. I had to give up my more confrontational style. And there was one more reason, which may have been the most important: I had met Hitoshi Ohashi, who would become my life partner.

I had no permanent job but I soon found consulting work with several organizations that were expanding in the United States, including Nissan, Hitachi, and NEC. I eventually added non-Japanese organizations such as AIG, the European Union, IBM, Intercontinental Hotels, Gap, and UBS to my client list.

After a year consulting in Japan, I started teaching part-time at a nearby university. I didn't know it at the time, but that institution, Keio University, is considered one of the best in Japan. More Japanese CEOs graduate from Keio than any other university in Japan,[1] and Keio ranks ninth in the world for the number of alumni holding CEO positions in Fortune Global 500 companies.[2] Eventually I was appointed to a full-time position and became the first tenured American full professor in the faculty of business and commerce.

When I left twenty-two years later, I gave my final lecture to three hundred people and the president of Keio University spoke to the group about how much I contributed to the university. I had to pinch myself— was he really talking about me? What happened? How did I do it? Work was working just as I had once dreamed it would.

I had learned how to make my life better and have a positive impact on the lives of the people I worked with. No one knew how much I had suffered in the past and how much time I had spent learning this different way.

I am still surprised when others tell me I am an inspiration. I didn't expect that, nor did I seek it out. I never set out to share some profound message with the world. In fact, I never set out to have any message at all. I was just trying to figure things out for myself. After all the time I spent learning about myself, doing so much research, and experiencing so many ups and downs, I had somehow developed a way of working that others were interested in.

This approach starts every day by focusing on what you want to create, a way of working that begins with the question that is the title of this book: *What Do You Want to Create Today?* This is the approach you'll learn in these pages. We'll begin in the same place I started: learning about yourself.

CHAPTER TWO

It's About You (Not Them)

Ken Sasaki was serious when he told me he wanted his life at work to be better. He was only thirty-seven and had what many would call success. Most people would think Ken had it made. We were sitting on thousand-dollar chairs around a huge mahogany table in the executive boardroom on the thirty-ninth floor of a new skyscraper. But Ken, the president of a large insurance company, wasn't happy.

He had an idea of what he wanted work to be, but this certainly wasn't it. Being a senior officer of this big international company looked good, but the way he saw it, work was one set of problems after another. It was late-night conference calls, inquiries from governmental regulating agencies, conferences with analysts to explain why profitability was up or down, streams of emails from headquarters all marked *urgent*. Some days things did slow down, but on those days he was bored and didn't know what to do with his time.

He told me he disliked the people he worked with too, even though he had hired most of them. He described many of them as too conservative or incompetent. In his opinion, his boss was the worst of all. Ken called him a "control freak," and even though his boss was in Singapore, Ken considered him a micromanager. Ken sat across from me, looked me straight in the eye, and said, "Work's got to be better than this." It was as if there were a dark cloud hanging over him preventing him from seeing clearly. I knew exactly what Ken was talking about. I had been very much like him.

Do you know anyone in this situation? I'll bet you do.

A Common Problem

There was a time when I would have been shocked by what Ken said, but not anymore. I meet people like him every day: bankers, lawyers, doctors, professors, entrepreneurs. They all have professional, respected jobs with good incomes—jobs that people around the world aspire to. But in their cases, the work isn't working out the way they want. They're too busy, they're hassled, they don't like their bosses, they're not challenged enough, there's too much pressure, they're not learning enough.

Put simply, work isn't working and they are not having the kind of lives they want. As you can imagine, they had all worked extremely hard, done well in college, and achieved a lot in their professional lives. Yet they could not escape a reckoning with their own sense of disillusionment.

Most were worried about what else they could do or what new actions they could take. In many cases, these successful professionals spoke in terms of confinement and fear. They say they "keep busy in order not to think," "can't sleep," "can't escape from worrying"; they "want to do something else"; or they love their job, it's their boss they hate. Others say they like the work, but it's the clients/the vendors/the employees who are driving them crazy.

I do not tell them to change jobs. That's not the answer. What I see over and over is that when these people change their jobs, within a year they're having the same kinds of problems in the new job as they had in the old one. Unless a person deals with the hard questions of who they are and who they want to be, the complaints start all over again. If you change your job without changing yourself, the result will be greater anxiety, unhappiness, and the same problems you tried to escape from.

I don't tell them to take a vacation either. That's the ultimate short-term response. I have clients who leave every weekend for time in the countryside or a long holiday at an expensive resort. "Work is hell," they tell me, "so I need to escape." As pleasurable as these places are, their trips are not so much for enjoyment as they are for forgetting the week. Why not develop a more satisfying way of working?

I also don't tell them, "Do what you have to do and the hell with your family." We all need people to support us, and we have to consider the impact of our decisions on our loved ones. Nor do I say, "Your boss is a jerk." We have to learn how to work with many different kinds of people. Part of our job is handling the boss, the clients, and the people with whom we work.

What I *do* tell them is that work can be a whole lot better. The first message I delivered to Ken (and hundreds like him I meet as an executive coach and conference speaker) was a tough one: The underlying problem lies within you. It starts with you, not anyone else.

It's not an easy notion for many people to accept. Can you? Let's find out.

I ask people the same questions I have asked myself. I ask them about the kind of life they want at work. I ask them to imagine what that would look and feel like to them. I ask them if they want to be having the same conversation with me a year from now. I ask them if they can let go of some of their ideas about what work has to be. I ask them what action *they* could take to break down some of the barriers to the kind of life they want at work. I listen to the answers without comment and then I ask even more questions.

Initially, it feels like I am not understanding the pain they feel. But eventually I see a different look on people's faces. And it's a look of understanding: Understanding the necessity of letting go of a strongly held belief about how they have to work. It may be letting go of an idea of what it means to be a leader, recognizing there are other ways to communicate with our bosses, or recognizing what is missing from work. Eventually, I see a look on their faces that shows they understand they are the ones who have to take action. Eventually, people recognize they have to shift their perceptions and actions and do something.

I know it is easy to get locked into seeing your situation as fixed, final, set in stone. Pema Chodron, the author and American Buddhist nun, tells this story of how hard it is to give up our views even in the face of compelling evidence: "A man's only son was reported dead in battle," she wrote. "The father locked himself in his house for three weeks, refusing all support and kindness. In the fourth week, the son returned home. Seeing that he was not dead, the people of the village were moved to tears. Overjoyed, they accompanied the young man to his father's house and knocked on the door. 'Father,' called the son, 'I have returned.' But the old man refused to answer. 'Your son is here, he was not killed,' called the people. But the old man would not come to the door. 'Go away and leave me to grieve!' he screamed. 'I know my son is gone forever and you cannot deceive me with your lies.'"[1]

So it is with all of us. We are certain we must continue our way of seeing and doing things, our truth. We too often think that our way of working and living is the only way. It's not. Breaking away will take some courage, some risk, and some tough work.

It Starts with You

I used to wonder why many people do not have the kind of life they want at work. They're smart. They have a solid skill set, a good education, money, graduate degrees. In fact, it looks like they are in the best situation possible. Shouldn't work be better? Shouldn't life be better? After all, work is such a big part of life.

But often these individuals think of their career first and postpone the long process of learning who they are. They have things backward. The first step for you to gain satisfaction in your career is to know yourself and know what you want.

I always ask new clients, "What do you want?" You'd be surprised at the long silences that typically follow that question. You'd think I was asking them to solve a complex math problem without a calculator, because the most frequent answer I get is, "I don't know. I don't know what I want."

In some cases, a client will say, "I know what I want, but I don't think I can ever have it," "My wife wouldn't let me do that," or, "I'll become homeless if I take that kind of job." It's a big question.

How about you? What do you want? What kind of life at work would you like to have?

When you answer, don't think about obstacles. It's time to think about what you really want. And it's never too late. "When is the best time to plant a tree?" an old Chinese proverb begins. "Twenty years ago and today." The same is true for you and your work.

In graduate school, I learned about a concept called "locus of control." Developed by psychologist Julian Rotter, locus of control means how you perceive the source of control within your own life. People with high locus of control believe they have high control of their lives. People with low locus of control believe that other forces and people control their lives.[2]

Locus of control refers to your beliefs and perceptions rather than what is really happening. If you believe that your promotion is based on external factors like luck or favoritism by your boss, this would show low locus of control. If you believe your promotion is based on your own effort and your relationships with others, this would show high locus of control. This is not an absolute measure. Think of it more as a scale where most of us would fall somewhere between the two extremes.

In my work, I have seen many people increase their locus of control and take greater charge of their own lives. It's possible to change your beliefs and widen your perceptions. One key is to detach from your current beliefs by living more in the moment. That's why I tell people to ask themselves, "What do I want to create today?" every day when they head to work.

I suggest they give some thought to what they want work to look like, what they want work to feel like. For example, if they've been having arguments with their boss, what different kind of relationship could they create. What could they change to make things better? One client of mine who loves to ski decided she would like to create a situation at work that looked like skiing. She would encounter "moguls" at work, but she would know how to handle them or maneuver around them, just like she did on the slopes.

Creating something today might also mean a single-minded focus on completing a report, preparing a PowerPoint presentation, or preparing a marketing plan. It could be beginning a friendship with a new coworker or building a stronger relationship with the boss. It might mean taking a step toward creating a better atmosphere at work by bringing pastries to the morning meeting or leaving your office door open as an invitation for others to come in and chat.

I suggest people answer the question for that day, right then, and think about what could happen now—not yesterday, not next week, but *now*. Try asking yourself what you would like to create today. You'll be surprised at the result, as long as you let yourself be open to the answer. Don't let yourself be trapped into obsessing about the boss or yesterday's awful client meetings or worrying about what you will do after retirement. Instead, ask yourself what you want to create today, right now, at this moment.

If the question *Do you know what you want?* is too tough to answer or appears too abstract, the question *Do you know what you want to create today?* will help you see what work could be. It's a small step, one that will help you figure out the answer to the bigger question of what you want.

Don't critique what you want or say it's impossible. Don't wait until you finish this book. Just say what you want. Write it down. Now.

Have you forgotten what you want? Many people have, or they've decided they can't obtain what they want, so they hide their real thoughts, feelings, and desires. Some are so busy just working away that they don't even think about what they want. Others fear that if they say what they want, they may set themselves up for disappointment if they cannot achieve it.

I'm always skeptical when I hear people say, "I don't know what I want." It comes out too easily. Often the person really does know what they want. Or at least they know what they once wanted.

It's easier not to acknowledge what you want, because with acknowledgment comes the responsibility of taking some action to achieve the goal. So, instead of declaring what they want, many people ignore and suppress what they want and simply say, "I don't know."

How about you? Do you find you're not being honest with yourself in this way? Are you really someone who "doesn't know"?

If the answer to what you want doesn't come to you right away, it can come to you over time. When working with my clients, I ask questions such as these to get closer to the answer:

- What's missing from the work you currently do?
- What do you like to do?
- What do you dislike doing?
- How would you like to work with your boss?
- Are there some images that come to mind when you think about the way you would like to work?

I don't ask clients to think about a specific job they want, but to think about what they would like *from* work and *at* work. Skill development? Joy? Fun? Respect? Independence? Accomplishment? Challenge? Who are the people you want to work with?

The answers eventually do come: "I want to work with my hands," "I'd like to help people," "I'd like to be more independent," "I'd like to have a more flexible schedule," "I want to handle my boss better," "I'd like to be more confident," "I want to use what I learned in business school."

I tell people to do some research, just like they once did in school or in other jobs. But this time the subject of their research is *themselves*.

To get what you want, you do not necessarily have to change jobs. You may be able to stay in the same job or with the same company by shifting your perspective or by transferring to another department. You may have to learn new skills for handling people, solving problems, or doing different tasks, but don't jump in right away with a to-do list. It's too early for that.

Does this idea of giving some serious thought to what you want speak to you? Have you been avoiding thoughts about what you really want? Is your first reaction, "I'm too busy to think about all this"?

Yet what could be more important?

It may seem that learning more about yourself is going backward rather than forward. But by learning about yourself, you are gaining insights that will give you the energy to have the kind of life at work you truly want.

You might wonder why you have to do this or why you can't just take a test that will tell you everything you need to know about yourself. Indeed, there are tests that will give you insight into yourself, but it's more important to develop the skills for observing yourself. Why let a test dictate the way you will live your life? Now is the time to develop self-observation skills you can use throughout your life.

I hear people say, "If only I had another boss, this job would be perfect." Yet once they get a new boss, things may be good for a while, but then I hear the same complaint: "My *new* boss is ruining my life at work." It's the same with money. "If only my salary were higher, I'd be happy." But then after a raise or two, their spending has increased beyond their new salary and they're wishing for even more money.

Having the kind of life you want at work has to do with only one person: you. Not your boss, not your spouse, not your family. Know about yourself and what you want first, and then it will be easier to deal effectively with your boss, spouse, and everyone else.

What to Do

Have you ever kept a daily journal or notebook? I have for more than thirty years, and it's been a helpful tool for learning. Dedicate a notebook or computer file to yourself. Write down what you're thinking about work and answer these questions, most of which I listed a few paragraphs ago:

- What's missing from the work you currently do?
- What do you like to do?
- What do you dislike doing?
- How would you like to work with your boss?
- Are there some images that come to mind when you think about the way you would like to work?
- Can you draw or describe these images?
- What do you want most of all?

When people ask me how they can become more successful at what they do, I always suggest they begin with self-knowledge. Here are several strategies I suggest that you too can use to learn about yourself.

1. Listen carefully to what people tell you.

"You are so creative," "You're so outgoing," "You look so happy," "You are really good with people; you'd make a great salesman." What do people say directly to you? These people are serious. You do not have to agree with what they say about you. But they are giving you valuable information. Appreciate it. When you get unsolicited comments, people are seeing something in you—something you may not even see yourself. It's not easy to change the way we see ourselves, but others can see something in us we do not even realize is there. Use your notebook or a computer file to write down what people are telling you.

Last week when I was introduced at a party, the host told one of the guests I was someone who knew beauty. I had never thought about myself that way even though I do own an art gallery. It was nice to hear this comment, and it made me think about myself in a different way. No doubt people say things about you that you may not have ever considered. Listen to them—and learn.

Some people have difficulty accepting compliments. If you're like that, you may be tempted to discount or dismiss the nice comments or disagree with them by saying, "That's not really true," or, "You are too kind." But resist doing so. Let it in. Just say, "Thank you."

Ditto for criticism. If people tell you, "You are defensive," "You have a short fuse," or, "You don't listen," accept it and thank them for the feedback. You can also ask for more information—"Why do you think I'm defensive?"—or ask for simple examples. You don't have to agree or disagree with them. Just be thankful you can get such feedback.

2. Go somewhere new, meet and see different people, do things you've never done before.

It's so easy to come up with the same programmed reactions and answers when you go to the same gym, the same restaurants, the same coffee shops. You're a creature of habit, like all of us.

Taking a job in Japan was an important step for me. Many of the clients I have worked with in Tokyo have told me the same thing. You go to a new place and meet new people and you feel less constrained. The responses and comments from people in your new place will be unencumbered and fresh. They will see you differently than your usual pals, and you'll uncover parts of yourself you may have kept hidden or didn't even know about.

Go to a culture that is very different, even for a visit, and you can see a lifestyle that may encourage you to look inside yourself. In Southern California I had what looked like a great life: a house by the beach, a good consulting practice, a BMW, a university position, some good friends. And I ran and swam almost every day.

I had the outside indicators of success, but inside there was something else going on. I spent a lot of time thinking about only one topic: status. I wanted more of it—to buy a bigger house, to drive a newer BMW, to open a bigger office. I focused on what other people thought rather than what I really wanted. The obsession with status was really a way of avoiding the truth. Like Ken at the beginning of this chapter, I didn't know what I really wanted.

I took a one-month break to try to figure things out. It wasn't a vacation, but a trip to learn more about myself and what I wanted. I went to Puerto Vallarta, Mexico. I spent time relaxing on the beach, exploring the sights, and watching the people. They looked happy, happier than the strivers I was hanging around with in Southern California. They didn't have much money, but they got enjoyment from walking along the ocean and being with their families and friends. I came back with a different perspective on how much money I needed to be happy. This was a trip with a purpose: to find out more about myself.

Next time you take a trip, travel for insight. Travel for self-discovery.

You also can learn about yourself by trying new things in your daily routine. This includes food. I call this *eating your way out of your comfort zone*. Try new foods and go to new restaurants. You may find that you like what you never thought you could possibly like. You'll meet new people and be encouraged to travel and learn more about other cultures. Learning about another way of life could push you to question assumptions about your career.

Try different sports, learn to dance, or read a book that typically wouldn't interest you. As I tried more new things, I discovered the enjoyment of riding on roller coasters and realized I wanted more excitement in my life. Now I even like the thrill of sitting up front in a roller coaster.

3. Pay attention to any physical reactions you have to people and to work.

Your body gives you information you can't ignore. You get a hangover or a headache if you drink too much. You get an upset stomach when you are under stress.

People often say their "stomach is in knots" when they're feeling nervous.

Notice what happens to your body when you're faced with certain types of tasks or dealing with certain people. Pay attention to these reactions.

Your body sends you strong, important messages. They all mean something. Does the thought of meeting new people make you sweat? Does looking at a pile of invoices make you shake? Do you feel like you've just been run over by a truck when you get off the phone with a certain person? Do you have a big smile on your face when you see certain colleagues? Do you get pumped up with adrenaline when you visit a factory to talk with young engineers?

When I asked one client, Stephen Cher., whether his body was giving him any messages, he told me he noticed it was becoming difficult to wake up in the morning to go to work. It wasn't because he was tired. He just didn't want to go in. He'd eventually get himself to the train station, but at least once a week he'd fall asleep on the train and pass the station where he was supposed to get off for his office. His body was sending him a message about his work.

4. Notice the people you attract.

Your friends and colleagues are often your mirror. You can see yourself in them. Are they active, energetic, happy, party animals, homebodies, movie lovers, creative, negative, boring?

What can you say about your friends? Take a look at them. Do you see yourself in them?

When I was teaching, my classes were always active, and by the end of the first month of the semester, the students would know almost everyone else in the class. At the end of each class session, they'd hang around to talk with me or make plans with each other to get something to eat, have a drink, or work on a project. It was interesting to see how the various informal groups formed. The more active students found each other; the ones who wanted to be entrepreneurs would also find one another. Even the ones who were falling behind and didn't know what was going on would band together.

Who are your friends at work? What do these choices say about you? Are your friends seen by others the way you would like to be seen? Is it time for some new friends, some different colleagues?

5. Meditate—it's the gateway to self-knowledge.

Meditation is not something only for people who chant and wear white robes. Meditation can help you learn about yourself. Meditation also reduces your stress levels, clears your mind, and lowers your heart rate.

You may want to learn a particular method of meditation, such as transcendental meditation or a type of meditation based on Buddhist or Indian principles. I've been meditating for more than thirty years. I need it to thrive. My style of meditation is my own, combined with visualization of what I want my day to look like. It ties in nicely with what I want to create every day. I let go of any stress I might feel. I relax. I clear my mind of any worries I might have. I think of how I want to go through my day. I push aside some of the problems that have been on my mind. I think of who I might see during the day and how I would like to deal with them.

If you'd like to learn an easy way to start meditating, I recommend *The Relaxation Response* by Herbert

Benson. You can learn what to do in a very short time, and if you practice for ten to twenty minutes twice a day, you will relieve your tension and gain a clear focus for your day, and, as Benson says on his book's back cover, obtain "a richer, healthier, more productive life."[3]

Meditation will give you greater peacefulness and a stronger connection to yourself. You'll be happier and more fulfilled, and you'll enjoy improved relations with people at work. It's no wonder there is a resurgent interest in meditation in Silicon Valley companies. Google, for example, offers meditation classes to its employees.

Often when I call a Boston-based friend of mine, I hear his voice mail announce, "I'm sorry I can't answer the phone now. I'm meditating. Please leave your message and I will get back to you." Meditation is clearly a priority for him.

Famed professional basketball coach Phil Jackson was also a great believer in the power of meditation. In his book *Sacred Hoops: Spiritual Lessons of a Hardwood Warrior,* Jackson talks about practicing Zen meditation, using the book *Zen Mind, Beginner's Mind* as his guide.[4] Make your mind clear, Jackson recommends, drawing on the Buddha's teaching in the Dhammapada: "Everything is based on mind, is led by mind, is fashioned by mind. If you speak and act with a polluted mind, suffering will follow you."[5]

If your thinking has been clouded with worries, or if you have been having trouble making a decision, meditation helps you clear away the clouds hanging over you. If you easily get caught up in arguments at work, meditation will help you stay calm and think before jumping in. When you meditate, you notice the thoughts that come into your mind and you quietly let them go.

6. Find a counselor or coach.

You can certainly learn about yourself on your own, but it will help if you can find someone to talk with about your process of self-understanding and self-realization. The learning will go deeper and faster too. You might think you can simply talk with your partner or best friend, but they aren't necessarily the best choices. They know you too well. They carry baggage about you, just as you carry baggage about them. They are likely to have a certain bias about what steps you should take. You need to choose someone who is not committed to a particular outcome, who isn't so familiar with you.

It was once very common for people to consult with trained therapists such as psychologists, psychiatrists, and family counselors. Today it seems to be more usual for people to work with a career coach or an executive coach.

Find someone who can support you as you learn about yourself. Whether you choose a psychologist, a counselor, or a coach, make sure you feel comfortable talking with that person. Do not choose someone who will push you into taking a new position or a certain belief system before you are ready. This is the time to think in terms of opening options, not closing them.

By learning more about yourself, you will strengthen your emotional intelligence so you'll be aware of the effects of other people on you and your effect on them. You'll be able to better match yourself to the type of work you do and the way you'd like to work. You will gain some insight into the changes you will need to make in order to have the kind of life you want. You'll also develop the confidence you need to make those changes.

In case you're wondering, you don't have to follow all of the methods I have detailed here simultaneously. Choose the ones that are most suitable for you. You can meditate, work with a counselor, listen to your friends—there's no set order, no prerequisites. By doing as many as you can when you can, you'll learn about yourself more quickly and more confidently.

Having the Life You Want at Work

Let's go back to some of the questions I raised earlier in this chapter. What does having that life at work look like for you? Is it working on your own schedule? Is it being respected by your peers? Is it having good relations with the people you work with? Is it about growing and learning? Is it about traveling? Is it about sharing what you know? Is it about making a contribution? Is it about having less stress?

Maybe visual images come to mind. Is it like surfing? Climbing a mountain? Being a warrior? Is it about wearing a suit or wearing shorts? Wingtips or flip-flops? Going to work in a limo or traveling by train?

If you could work in this new way, how would your life be better?

As a consultant, I often go to offices and watch the way people work. I observe meetings, interview people, and sometimes I just hang around in the employee lunchroom. That's one place where I can really under-stand a company's culture.

I like to watch how people come and go and walk around the office. Are people happy when they see each other? Do they complain when they talk? Do they blow off steam? Do they laugh? Do they yell at each other?

I always like to find the person in every organiza-tion who, no matter what is going on, manages to keep his or her cool and not be undone by the next turn of events. This person always interests me. This is the kind of person I wanted to be.

In your office, is there a person like this? Would you like it to be you?

In Japan, I set out to be the kind of professor who would make a difference in other people's lives. I had a dream of what I wanted to do, and that's what I set out to do. I remembered the best teachers I had in high school and the best professors I had at Boston Univer-sity and the University of Massachusetts, and I wanted to be like those people.

I also wanted to have good relations with colleagues and peers. I wanted to avoid the kind of in-fighting that had almost sunk my career before. I remembered the charged political environment of universities where I had taught in the United States, filled with late-night hushed phone calls and secret tenure votes. When I started in Japan, I focused more on what I wanted to contribute. I didn't set out to be popular. I wanted to be the kind of professor people would remember.

How about you in your work? Is there something unique, something valuable, you can contribute? Will people remember you? If so, how will they remember you? Think more about your eulogy than your résumé.

As the first American full-time professor at Keio University, I knew all eyes would be on me. My actions were scrutinized, but I looked at it as a great opportunity because I could influence how others saw Americans. I could break any stereotypes other faculty members might have had, and I could follow my own path.

I didn't know any of the rules of Japanese society or Japanese universities, and I could stake out my own way of doing things. Being an outsider can be a real asset. I was inspired by the story of an outsider who made a real difference through his presence alone.

As a young consultant, I worked with the Boston Public Schools helping to integrate schools that previously had been predominantly white or black Integration meant redrawing district lines and busing students to schools across town to achieve a more equitable balance of white and black students. There was much opposition to this desegregation that was ordered by the courts. Every day there were violent protests.

Teachers and administrators were afraid for their lives because of bomb threats and Molotov cocktails being hurled at the schools. Many employees felt the senior administrators lacked the will and ability to lead them through the crisis. And then rumors started flying that a new leader, Bob Wood, would soon be leading the Boston Public Schools.

Dr. Robert Wood had been the U.S. secretary of housing and urban development and the president of the University of Massachusetts, and now he was to be superintendent of the Boston Public Schools. The job had been previously held by political appointees, many of whom were considered incompetent and not fully committed to integration.

And then even before Bob Wood arrived, there seemed to be a transformation in the school head-quarters where I was consulting. Almost to a person, the teachers, administrators, and staff, all of whom had once looked beaten-down and defeated, now stood taller and prouder, knowing they were about to have a leader who would make a difference. The staff started talking about how they wanted to make integration succeed. They showed up for work on time and stayed late. Even before he was officially sworn in, Bob Wood was an instrument of change because of his reputation, because of who he was. He was the message.

Many wondered why he would want the job, but he saw the superintendent position as an opportunity to make a real difference in the city where he lived. His ability to influence was not because of his PhD. It was not because he had taken any course on changing large-scale organizations. It was not because he was coming in with a "change program." It was just him; he could get things moving even before his first day. He came in to do a job and that's exactly what he would focus on. And best of all, people knew it.

Do you know anyone who has that kind of impact by virtue of their presence alone, by just showing up?

Seeing Bob Wood's ability to move people because of who he was motivated me to become such a person. It was seeing what Bob Wood could do even before he started his job that propelled me to become someone who could influence others. Gandhi is often quoted as saying, "You must be the change you want to see in the world."[6] I took that slogan as my own.

Who you are is more important than the degrees you have. The degrees might get you a job, but that's not what will help you get things done. Nor will these degrees keep you engaged in the work you do. I've seen students and clients pay money to earn more and more certificates to add to their portfolios and résumés, but I recommend building a strong foundation of self-knowledge first before adding to your list of certificates. There is no end to the degrees or skills you can accumulate without doing what is most important: connecting to yourself.

All of that time I spent looking at the faculty catalogs I wrote about in the first chapter of this book made me realize it's not the degrees that make the difference. It's you. Of course, you need a specific level of education for certain jobs. You can't be a lawyer without a law degree, and many businesses will not hire you unless you're a college grad. But it's you, not your degrees, that will make you effective.

There is an obsession worldwide with obtaining more certificates and degrees and adding more skills to your résumé. Go to the gates outside any university campus in Japan and you will see a small army of people handing out flyers to undergraduate students. The flyers advertise cram schools for job hunting, classes for job interviews, schools for taking the Graduate Record Exam or the GMAT, or for becoming a CPA. And there are professors and counselors who will tell the students they should take as many of those courses and classes as they can.

There is nothing wrong with having these skills and certificates, but when I'm asked if they're a good idea and are necessary, I simply say, "Know what you want first." That's the place to start.

How about you?

What do you want work to be?

What do you want to create at work?

What if you looked at work in a different way?

What if you looked at work as a place where you could make the dreams of your life come true?

What if you focused on the kind of life you would like to have at work?

What if you looked at work as a blank canvas where you could paint part of your life?

Think you are too busy? What could be more important than making the changes that would make your life better?

Maybe you think it's impossible to think about what you really want because you've invested so much time in the job you currently have, or because you have just started out in your career. Maybe you think it's impossible because you worry about what others will say. Or it's impossible because you count on that big salary and you think you will lose it if you make a change.

But it's not impossible. You might even earn more money. You need to give some serious thought to what you want. All it will take is time and the determination to make work better using your own resources—your personality, your character, your actions.

What action can you take that will help you have the kind of life you want at work today? What can you change about the way you work?

Nelson Mandela knew that if he were to lead the people of South Africa, he could not set himself apart from others. That included the way people referred to him. When I saw him being interviewed on TV, he told the interviewer, "Call me Nelson. That's what I prefer." I thought, *How amazing, how wonderful. The great Nelson Mandela goes by his first name.*

On that day, I decided to no longer signal to students that I wanted to be called doctor or professor or mister. When classes started again, I just wrote "Bob Tobin" on the board. No titles. No degrees. I didn't lose any stature or prestige. I signaled to my students from day one that the class and the professor would be accessible to them. It was simple.

As I was becoming the kind of professor I wanted to be, some colleagues were curious about what I was doing in class, and I extended an open invitation to them to visit. None did. One friend who taught at another university was always looking for ways to put some excitement in his teaching. His course was on trade regulations, and he would go over the intricacies of each of the laws with the students. He'd tell me how he wanted to change how he taught and he'd ask for teaching suggestions.

"Why not have students research the laws and then present them?" I asked him. "Great idea," he said. But he worried the students might be uncomfortable and would not explain some of the laws clearly. I told him he could encourage the students, make corrections, or offer a summary.

But again he hesitated, and continued to teach in the same way. He came back the following year and told me once again that the students were so quiet and didn't participate. I gave him a few more ideas, but eventually we stopped meeting. Although he perceived the barrier to be the students, the real barrier was him.

And the same is true for all of us. It's not about them. It's really about us. And taking action requires courage and confidence to do things differently. I'll talk about both concepts in other chapters of this book.

But first, let's talk about your dreams.

CHAPTER THREE

Dreams Have Soul; Objectives Don't

I don't understand why people think their dreams are something for later, something for when they retire. Retirement is not a guarantee, especially in these economic times. Why wait until life expectancy is at its shortest to begin to live fully? Do they think they will live forever? A person's life can be cut short in an instant, and their dreams die with their last breath.

That's why I always ask new clients about their dreams. It's your dreams that connect to your soul and your spirit. Paraphrasing the words of Henry David Thoreau, "Go confidently in the direction of your dreams! Live the life you've imagined."[1]

It's rare for people to talk about their dreams in these terms, or even talk about their dreams at all. Usually people label their dream as something narrower, like attaining a specific income level, becoming a CEO, or buying a Mercedes-Benz. But those are not the dreams I am talking about. Dreams are bigger. The dreams I mean are those aspirational thoughts about how your life could be when your work aligns with your values. I define a dream as what a person wants for his or her life, including career, lifestyle, place, and values.

Jared Chan, my new client in Hong Kong, was trying to figure out what to do next in his life. He was thirty-six, a graduate of one of the top business schools in America. He had trained as an architect in Australia and was recruited by high-tech firms in Silicon Valley. He stayed with a well-known company there for six years after business school. After he quit, he got in touch with me.

"I just couldn't do it anymore," he told me. He didn't even stick around for his bonus, which would have been $20,000. He told me that having his life back was worth more than that. He didn't want to stay in the high-tech industry, and he wasn't sure he wanted to be an architect either.

When we sat down to talk, I asked him specifically about his *dreams*. I didn't ask him about his dream *job*, like so many headhunters had asked before. That's different. I wanted to know what he wanted for his life, what values were important to him, what aspirations he had. It took him a while to think, but he told me he really wanted to do something much more creative.

Jared wanted to use everything he knew. He didn't want to work every day either. He'd be very happy if he could help in the preservation of old buildings in Yogyakarta, Singapore, and other places in Asia going through major redevelopment. He didn't want to see all the old buildings replaced by high-rises. He could help with design and preservation. He knew several languages. He also wanted to get back into hiking and mountain climbing. These were his dreams, and I encouraged him to go toward them.

Over the course of the next several months, he made connections in the region and he flew to Jakarta and Yogyakarta in Indonesia and George Town and Kuala Lumpur in Malaysia. He took some design work with a consultancy based in Singapore and began to make his dreams come true. In an email I got from him recently, he told me he had never been happier in his life and his work. He felt he was working with his head and his heart. He said he hadn't thought it was possible to connect his life and his career, but now he was happily living his dream. His story is the kind I love to hear: stories of people who are making their dreams for their lives come true.

I always make dreams a part of my discussion with new clients. I did the same with students. On the first day of class, I always asked my students about their dreams. Many would say that a dream was something for the future, but I encouraged them—and I want to encourage you—to think of a dream as something for *now*.

Give some thought now to your own dreams. Write them down. Don't be shy about declaring your dreams, and don't be so quick to judge your dreams and say "impossible." They may be more possible than you think. There is no end to the number of people who will tell you you're not being realistic. Listen to them at your peril. Ignore a big portion of what these naysayers tell you.

Marc Le Menestrel, a business professor at Universitat Pompeu Fabra in Barcelona, sees dreaming as a useful tool that can connect our personal lives to our business lives. He has found that people often dream of being part of a community that reflects their values, and of contributing to the lives of other people in some way.

Le Menestrel has found that our dreams can help us in maintaining motivation, taking a long view, and staying flexible. When you keep your dream alive, you are not easily discouraged, you figure out how to deal with obstacles, and you're able to adapt. Le Menestrel knows how goals can be confining and limiting: "You want to be the master of your goal," he says, "not the prisoner of your goal."[2]

Goals at Work

The goals and objectives you have at work or the monetary goals you have set for yourself are not the same as dreams. Goals and objectives are those achievements to which you are directing some effort, something your efforts are intended to attain. They are often work-related, such as improving the accuracy rate in entering orders online, increasing sales, or reducing legal fees. They are set for you, or you set them jointly with your manager.

Goals do work in helping individuals accomplish tasks. Many studies show how goals drive behavior and improve performance. They certainly work for athletes, for salespeople—in fact, for all highly competitive people. But there are negative aspects to goal setting as well, and often these are ignored. You can imagine that in the rush to achieve goals, individuals may ignore their own ethical principles, and they may focus too narrowly.

When you work in a company that has a goal-setting program, you may have little choice but to follow these prescribed measures of success or failure. You need to attend to those goals if you want to keep your job and advance in the company. But do not lose track of your dreams. Too many people forget their dreams and blindly follow a path they do not fully embrace.

It's ideal when the goals you have at work are aligned with the dreams you have for your life. When the goals and objectives have little meaning for you, consider what you are giving up to achieve these goals. It could be something as important as your life. You may be willing to put what you really dream of on hold for a short while, but when ignoring your dreams becomes a long-term pattern of behavior, it will be impossible for you to create the kind of life you want at work. You may dream of doing work that will help people become physically fit, for example, yet you work in a very sedentary customer service job where you continue to gain weight and eat at your desk. What's happened to your dream?

What's Wrong with Goal Setting?

Managers usually rave about setting goals and the process of setting them, but goals and objectives can actually be harmful to the individual and to the organization. Several university researchers, including Max Bazerman at Harvard Business School, have found that these harmful aspects include an overly "narrow focus that neglects non-goal areas, a rise in unethical behavior, distorted risk preferences, corrosion of organizational culture, and reduced intrinsic motivation."[3]

In an article in Harvard Business School's *Working Knowledge*, two examples stand out. The first is that Bausch & Lomb employees falsified financial statements to meet earnings goals. Second, that Ford knowingly designed a car that was vulnerable in rear-end collisions in the effort to meet pricing and weight goals. Adam Barsky of the University of Melbourne, another researcher cited in the article, is quoted as saying that "focusing on goals actually distorts our perception of what is unethical behavior."[4]

In my own consulting practice, I have coached executives in companies where environmental impact statements were manufactured in order to meet acceptable levels. I've also witnessed sales executives load up clients with machinery they didn't need in order to meet a sales quota. The customers were burdened with the financial obligation of paying for the equipment, the sales reps had trouble meeting the next year's quota, and the image of the supplier suffered.

A single-minded focus on goals robs your work of meaning and connection to your life. In the rush to reach your goals, you can begin to feel as if you are more machine than human. That is why dreams are so important.

Even the dreams you have about what you do outside of work can keep you engaged at work. An animal lover, for example, could dream and devote his time after work to rescuing abandoned and abused dogs and cats. And this mission could be what keeps him productive and engaged at work.

In some organizations, goal setting can be a colossal waste of time. I have attended and conducted many workshops where people spend hours setting goals and

developing action plans, only to have everything dis-
carded after the direction of the company changes or
a new leader is appointed. Even more frequent are the
times that the goals and plans get lost and dusty in
a bottom drawer as the whole goal-setting process is
forgotten.

A growing number of researchers, including Sam
Culbert of UCLA, believe the entire process of goal
setting and performance evaluation should be scrapped
and replaced with a performance culture where people
collaborate.[5] Max Bazerman of Harvard agrees. As an
alternative to goal setting, he suggests creating an environment where people want to achieve. He states that
organizations ignore the potential of intrinsic motivation as a way of moving toward achievement.[6] Harvard
administrators never set goals for him. He worked for
himself, for his own goals, and to advance the scholarship in his field. It was the same for me in my work at
Keio University.

Goals are so ingrained in business that it's hard
to get people to think of any other way to accomplish
anything. Managers say the process itself is valuable. Maybe it is, but there is so much disappointment when the goals are scrapped or not reached
that people's energy and commitment wanes. "We
change direction every time the leaves fall," is what
I heard twenty years ago in companies. Now what
I hear is, "We change direction every time we get a
new executive."

Many companies, including Adobe Systems with
14,000 employees, are in fact scrapping the entire performance appraisal and goal-setting process. As an
alternative, the managers give more regular feedback.

Without the drama of performance appraisals, I expect there will be higher morale and lower turnover.

When I caught up with a friend recently in an airport lounge, he told me how nervous he was about an upcoming performance appraisal. I understood, of course, since most people are understandably anxious about performance appraisals. But he wasn't the one being appraised; he was the one conducting the appraisals of people reporting to him.

Why continue a system that creates such a high level of anxiety for both parties and does not necessarily increase productivity? Add to this all the time it takes, and you have a system that doesn't work and that may adversely affect the bottom line. And yet it continues.

Knowing and Declaring Your Dream

After a recent talk I gave in Taipei, a young man told me he really appreciated what I said about dreams. In his company, no one ever talked about the future. No one ever asked him about his dreams.

"They only talk about the past, about achievements, about goals reached or not reached, about KPOs [Key Performance Objectives]," he told me. He liked the prestige of working for a well-known company, but he felt as if he were alienated from what he wanted for his life. He was beginning to think his only reason for being was to reach his goals.

You may be evaluated and given salary increases based on your level of goal attainment. But never forget your dreams. Make a plan for achieving them. Not someday, but today. This is what will propel you toward creating the life you want. This is what will motivate you. This is what will keep you moving forward when you encounter obstacles that are the natural part of life. These dreams are for creating something that is uniquely you.

My own dreams include seeing people more engaged in their work, creating and achieving their own dreams, and happier and more satisfied with what they are doing. My dream is to make a positive difference in the lives of others. I would like to see you too work with power, passion, and purpose.

As a professor, I wanted to be the kind of teacher students would remember. My dream was to be as good as the best professors I had in my own university life. I wanted to have a positive influence on young people as they started their careers. I wanted to encourage young people to dream bigger dreams.

I never made it my goal to get all high-level evaluations on the assessment forms the university gives students to complete at the end of each semester. I could get all high marks and the work itself could be meaningless to me. The evaluation form rates the professor on "reasonable assignments," "comes to class on time," "rarely lets class out early," and other measures that were not my own. I focused instead on achieving my own dream of being a great professor. And I still got excellent teaching evaluations.

What about the goals and objectives you set and the evaluations you receive at work? Do they fit with your dreams? Is focusing on your goals and your performance reviews killing your dreams, making you focus on measures that are unimportant to you, or pushing you to make some unethical moves?

My dream now in writing this book is to get my message out. I want to change the way people work. I want people to have more meaning from work. I want people to be happier at work. I want people to be able to handle the challenges they face at work. This is the dream that keeps me writing. As a writer, I don't set daily word-count objectives. Instead, I dream about writing something today that will help people make positive changes in their lives.

In the art gallery too, which I run with my partner, I dream about enriching people's lives by placing art in their homes and offices. I dream about the artists in our gallery developing international reputations. These are the kinds of things that push me in new directions in my work. And these dreams help me when I face obstacles or disappointments in my work.

When a gallery visitor comes in and says, "My four-year-old could paint that," or a potential client comes in and looks at forty paintings and tells me, "I don't like any of these," I don't let myself get discouraged, because I focus on my bigger dream.

On those days when you may not feel like doing very much and you lose your motivation to work, it's not money or goals that will motivate you to get back at it. It's not fear either. These don't work for many people for very long. Try instead to connect with something big like the dreams you have for your life and the reasons you work.

About every six months, I get a group email from a corporate lawyer friend who apologizes for being out of touch and tells me how busy he has been. He writes something noncommittal like, "Hope to get together with you soon." But he never does make further contact.

As long as I have known him, he's been either working 24/7 or escaping on a holiday. He stays in his jobs for a maximum of two to three years and then he takes a few months to recover. Each time he takes a new job, he says he is going to work "more like a human this time," but it doesn't take long before he's caught up in the same alternating patterns of intensive work coupled with total escape.

When I do run into him, he tells me he's "too old to be working like this." He apologizes for never having time to socialize. He shocks me when he says he hopes he'll get fired so he can slow down—as if that would solve the problem. It won't. He needs to make a deliberate effort to make changes in the way he works. But nothing changes, and I expect I will be hearing the same story for a while, which brings to mind another benefit of focusing on your dreams: They attract others.

Your dreams will bring people with similar dreams into your life. You'll find the best people for you. You'll meet people whose dreams are aligned with yours and you'll meet them as friends in your organization. You'll meet people who are *doing* things rather than *talking about* doing things. We'll explore having the best people in your life in a future chapter, but for now just remember that your dreams help you connect with people whose dreams align with yours.

The Case of Jeff Rowe

Not too long ago, I coached Jeff Rowe, a marketing section head for a global cosmetics company. He was experiencing a great deal of stress related to reaching his monthly targets. He was forty-two and consistently missing his performance goals at work. He was also single with no time to date. He hadn't taken a vacation in four years. Topping it all, he was in danger of getting fired.

Whenever he was away from the office, he worried that he should be working more to achieve his goals. He stayed at the office late, brought work home with him, and spent a good deal of time on the weekends developing strategies for increasing the success of his products. In short, his whole life was being spent obsessing about his goals.

He was spinning his wheels, not succeeding, and was always afraid to do anything outside of work that might take him away from those goals. I wondered how he could possibly do effective work when he was feeling such great anxiety. His worries about achieving were getting in the way of him doing his job. He was lost in a cloud of worry.

I didn't suggest that he work harder. I didn't suggest he revise his target. I asked him about his dream. He told me it was to reach his objectives. I hear this response a lot from people, but that is not a dream, nor is buying a condo or a Rolex.

I asked him again about his dream in a few different ways: "What would you like to accomplish? What would you like to see happen as a result of your work?" After a lot of thought, he told me, "I'd like to help people look as beautiful as they possibly could. I'd like people to take better care of their skin." He also told me he'd "like to have a well-balanced life, to get married, and have a family."

Those are dreams, and I asked him to keep those in mind.

Second, I suggested that he write down his worries and hide them somewhere in his office. They'd be there if he needed them. If he started worrying during the day, I suggested he gently push his worries away. It's not possible to think of new strategies and ideas if you are consumed by worry.

Third, I suggested he go home every day by 6 P.M. and start going out and enjoying life. I was sure if he were working less, he'd find some time to date.

Jeff looked at me as if I were nuts. He didn't like my ideas, and he told me so. But he was willing to try them because I was highly recommended by another executive in his company and he was desperate.

It took him awhile, but he stopped worrying so much after he wrote his worries down. A few months later during one of our meetings, he took out his worries list and laughed. "I can't believe I was worried about these things."

He started going home from work early and was soon dating. He lost twenty pounds, bought some new clothes, and got a fancy haircut. He had a lot more time to think of effective marketing strategies, and some of the best people in his company starting helping him. He developed a lot of internal interest in his products. He kept his dreams alive in his mind, and that motivated him to move forward. He came up with new ideas for selling and marketing his products. He got ideas from the movies, museums, and stores he visited with the women he dated. The goals really did take care of themselves. And he surpassed them within the next three months.

The Pressure to Create Goals

It's hard to resist creating goals for your work even if you work by yourself. Goals, after all, are an important part of the language of business. I often felt a bit embarrassed about not writing down my own goals. My friends and clients are surprised when I tell them I don't set goals. They mistakenly think I am not ambitious or not very well organized. But I have my dreams and they are what propel me forward, keep me moving ahead, keep me motivated, and give meaning to my work.

There are those times when I feel almost guilty about not setting goals. I then sit myself down and come up with goals: how much income I want, how many billable days, how many new clients I need to get. I develop a whole action plan. In the beginning I feel so good, as if I have some direction.

"Wow, now I know what I am doing, where I'm going," I say to myself. I get out there and go to networking events and send out articles and hustle to reach my objectives. But the whole process seems so hollow to me. And it seems to demean my whole way of working with people. Do I want to work with them because I could add some value and the project is interesting, or do I want to work with them just to reach my goals?

Then, out of the blue, I'll get a call from a former client and be offered a good-size consulting project. I'll forget about the goals I had set. The financial goals take care of themselves. As with all those people struggling to set goals in big companies, my own goals go right out the window.

Goals Can Crush Your Dreams

One of my first consulting jobs was working as a techni-
cal adviser and curriculum developer for a large project
designed to improve career development programs in
the country's vocational schools. I wanted desperately
to succeed. And I had my dream. I wanted to improve
schools throughout the United States. Part of my job
was visiting schools around the country and finding out
what they needed to excel. After these site visits, I'd be
so charged up I'd go back to my office, confer with colleagues, and write up a storm. I was motivated by my
desire to make a difference in public education.

The project was on schedule, even ahead of schedule. The whole team worked more than sixteen hours
a day, often six days a week to complete the project.
When my boss left to work on another project in Europe
for a month, I had hoped those of us working together
would be able to manage ourselves. But a new boss was
brought in, and his idea of leadership was to assign each
of us a goal to produce a certain number of pages every
day. He would collect our work at the end of the day. I
doubt if he ever read what we wrote.

This completely changed our motivation. Now we
were working for a quota instead of working in pursuit
of a dream. We really resented this way of being man-
aged. The temporary boss never met with us, never gave
us any feedback, but simply kept a checklist to make
sure we reached our quotas.

We did meet the goals he set, but for so many of
us on the team, the desire to do great work, to make a
contribution to education, was gone. These goals and

the monitoring systems that supported them almost ruined our dream, and some people left the project and the company. They didn't want to work for an organization that did not understand their dreams. As I think back on this experience, I am sure the quality of the work suffered as well since we had such a focus on making the quota without any quality measures. I believe now that I could still have focused on my dreams despite the overbearing management style, but at that time the single-minded focus on goals had a very negative impact on my dreams and my motivation.

A singular focus on goals in organizations is often an indication of a lack of trust. Goals are developed more easily than trust. When there is trust in an organization, there is less need for goals and elaborate systems for monitoring those goals.

What purpose do goals serve where you work? Do people talk about dreams? Are there steps you could take to restore trust, strengthen relationships, and work in a more collaborative way?

Losing Track of Dreams

It takes courage and determination to hold on to your dreams, or even to create your dreams. It's much easier to focus on goals or be continuously preoccupied with problems.

A university colleague of mine continually asked me for advice on how to handle the simplest of situations. She was in her fifties and shouldn't have been knocked over by the normal ebb and flow of university life, but she had a hard time dealing with the political maneuverings found in every university.

One time I asked her if she would give some thought to what she really wanted to accomplish as a professor—that is, what her dream was. Her answer: "That's too difficult for me to think about. Can you just help me handle this situation?"

My friend Linda is someone who always sets goals but whose goals don't serve her. She is an independent consultant, and every time I meet her she tells me she is tired of the work she is doing. She wants to do something besides consulting and management training. She wants to do something that is more uniquely suited to her. She tells me she'd like to do more speaking and more writing. Her dream is to create a center for executive retreats in Penang, Malaysia. She wants to use what she knows about executive development, yoga, food and nutrition, and psychology to create a beautiful space for executives to recharge.

But she never moves on this. I'm not sure what keeps her stuck, but for some reason Linda never moves in the direction of her dreams. Instead, she focuses on goals. She sets goals for amount of income and number of new clients. She takes on management training work that doesn't interest her in order to meet her goals. Her worst nightmare, she tells me, is to continue doing management training. She tells me she is bored, that she will make her dream come true "someday," but I've known her for ten years, and I always hear the same story.

Once I confronted her and asked, "When?" and she got upset with me. She said she was too busy with her goals to focus on her dreams right now. Instead of her goals serving her, she is serving her goals. She could set goals related to her dream, but for some reason she does not.

There are many excuses for delaying thinking about your dreams and taking action in pursuit of them, but you will only be postponing the life you want.

Your Dreams and Goals

Make your dreams something that will give your life meaning, something that you can reasonably achieve. Don't say, "I want to win the French Open/join the Bolshoi." It's not going to happen unless you began on a very different path when you were around the age of six. Think about the kind of life you want to live and declare it. Declaring your dream can be the simple first step in eventually making your dream come true.

I dreamed for many years of being a columnist. I wanted to share my views with a wider audience than I would meet in classes and in consulting. I told people I wanted to be a columnist and sent sample columns to many newspapers and magazines in the United States and in Japan. I was able to sell individual articles to several publications but never could sell the idea of a regular column.

But things have changed dramatically in the publishing world. Today you don't need a publication to write a column. You can write your own column on your own blog. And that's what I did. I created my blog, drbobtobin.com, and used it to get my ideas out there.

That was really enough, and I could now call myself a columnist, even if it was on my own blog, but after writing my column for a few months, I got an email from a friend who was an editor for an online publication asking me if I would be willing to write a weekly column. Of course I said yes. My dream came true and I could *really* call myself a columnist. I declared my dream, let others know about my dream, and my dream came true.

Considering your dreams more important than goals flies in the face of much of the advice we get in school, from our families, and at work. I know consultants and coaches who work like personal fitness trainers. They sit down with clients, set up a list of goals and objectives, and then meet every week to review progress toward those goals and objectives.

I question how many people really need that level of monitoring. I wonder how many adults need to be trained like a young child. I wonder how many children even need this. Do you? What happens when the monitoring stops? I'd be willing to bet that if you are reading this book, you don't need that kind of supervision.

Learning from Finland's Education System

Schools have become obsessed with setting objectives and testing, but the lessons from the Finnish education system are making some educators question whether this obsession with objectives and testing is really worth it. Finland scored first in science and second in reading and math worldwide on the standardized test administered by the Program for International Student Assessment.[7] Finnish students take only one mandatory standardized test, at age sixteen. Finland's achievement gap between the weakest and strongest students academically is the smallest in the world.[8] Since it implemented huge education reforms more than forty years ago, Finland's school system has consistently been at the top of the international rankings.[9]

Finland goes against the evaluation-driven, centralized model that much of the Western world uses. Teachers are trusted. They can do whatever it takes to make the students succeed.[10] According to an article in the *New York Times*, "Finland scorns almost all standardized testing before age sixteen and discourages homework. It is seen as a violation of children's right to be children to start school any sooner than the age of seven."[11] This seems like such a humane way of teaching children. Why shouldn't our work provide the same level of respect and trust?

Those Never-Ending Monetary Goals

Two years ago, I consulted with the president of a hedge fund in Korea. He grew the business quickly, but there was a lot of employee turnover and a high level of tension in the offices. It was not unusual to hear him yelling at subordinates and then to hear his direct reports yelling at their teams.

I was there to help him lead more effectively and help develop his executive team. He was only thirty-three and bragged that he had personally saved $17 million. But it wasn't enough for him. He fired a few of his assistants right before the company's Christmas party in order to increase his own pay. His own father berated him for not giving any money to the hospital that saved his son's life after a serious accident.

He told me he'd slow down and return to "being human" once he had $20 million in the bank. For him, money was everything. He focused only on the number. He had his goal but no dream. Focusing on the monetary goal robbed him and others around him of their humanity. I encounter similar, if less extreme, examples every day.

Where does the striving stop? And who will stop it if you don't?

No doubt you've heard people complain that once they reach one set of goals at work, their boss just raises the bar higher and higher. In certain "thankless" organizational cultures, no matter what is achieved, no one is thanked or congratulated. The reward is often higher goals devoid of meaning to your own dreams and life.

Go in the direction of your dreams. In the next chapter, we'll talk about a skill called "reading the air" that will propel you closer to those dreams.

CHAPTER FOUR

You Have to Read the Air

Kosuke Yamagata couldn't wait to tell me the good news. After fifteen years as president of the Japan branch of a European engineering company, he was going to be appointed to the global board of directors. I was surprised to hear this, but I didn't hesitate to congratulate him.

It had been a rough road for Kosuke in this company. He had fought with the company's CEO and several VPs of international operations over strategy and about keeping the Japanese division of the firm independent.

Kosuke took the appointment to the board as a sign that he was now going to be listened to and the company would soon follow *his* direction. "I'll shape up the board," he told me, "and they'll finally give the Japan division the respect it deserves."

I wasn't so sure. The chairman ran the board with a heavy hand. I knew many of the board members from my consulting work with this company, and they did nothing more than rubber-stamp the decisions of the chairman. The chairman owned 60 percent of the stock and liked to brag about how he never went to college, but now ran a huge engineering firm.

I told Kosuke I didn't think he was appointed to "shape up the board" when I sat down with him for our weekly coaching session. The following week, he would go to New York to attend his first board meeting as a board member. He had prepared elaborate charts about the new global strategy he was going to propose. He wanted me to go over them with him. "What do you think?" he asked.

I told him that his tenure on the board of directors might be the shortest in the company's history if he went ahead and presented any of the materials he had there. "Leave the charts at home," I told him. "Before you do anything or present any information, you have to read the air."

"What do you mean?" he asked. "I wouldn't have been appointed unless they wanted change." I told him he couldn't be so sure. I explained that before he did anything, he had to understand the environment of the board. He had to know how things worked there. He had to pay attention to *things he couldn't see*. He had to see the way the board operated, the way the board conducted its business, the way board members worked with each other, and how open they would be to his suggestions. That's what I mean when I say "reading the air."

"You may know how to get things done in Japan, where you are the boss," I told Kosuke, "but things are done differently at the board level, and you have to understand how everything's done there first." Again,

I said, "Read the air—New York is not Tokyo, and the global board of directors is a very different kind of team. You have to learn about new situations before you take any definite action."

Kosuke knew about reading the air because many Japanese people actually do so, but in his excitement about what he saw as this opportunity to change corporate strategy, he had forgotten all about it. That's what happens when people want things to happen quickly.

Reading the air is essential to having the kind of life you want at work. It means understanding the environment or the situation based on things you usually can't see but can feel. It also saves your career from sudden death. It's a necessary ingredient in being more effective in what you do and in helping you reach your dreams. And not just in Japan.

Organizations are often very bureaucratic places. The typical firm may appear to be a stone wall closed to ideas and innovation. In places where people may not speak out, reading the air is especially important. You have to assess the situation first and then act accordingly. Put another way, you have to find out where the loose stones might be in the stone wall. That will show you where you can push with the most success.

The late C. K. Prahalad of the University of Michigan and Gary Hamel of London Business School first discussed the idea of finding loose stones in the wall in their classic article on strategic intent in *Harvard Business Review*.[1] But finding the loose stones need not be limited to business strategy. It's an important element in having the kind of life you want at work. You have to find those soft spots, the low-hanging fruit that indicates readiness for change.

When you can read the air, you don't have to ask if it's okay to do something, you don't ask for permission, and you don't follow the rules. Sometimes you make the rules; sometimes you break the rules. And you know which rules to break. It's your reading of the air that enables you to know what to do to get things done.

What Is Reading the Air in Practice?

It's your keen observation skills that help you read the air. Here are some questions that can help: Are people timid or bold about making suggestions? Are they formal or informal when talking with each other? Are there some "undiscussables"? Are certain topics considered too personal? Is anyone smiling? Do people look too serious? Are people having long conversations in secret? Who speaks up at meetings? Where do people hang out? Can you tell who the boss is by the way people treat her or him?

The closest expression in English is "understanding the culture or the situation," but this doesn't quite do it justice. Reading the air focuses on what you can't see but can feel and notice—with some practice.

You will need to use all of your senses to know what people are feeling, to know what is happening in a group, and to understand what is not spoken clearly. This means developing and trusting your powers of observation, and it means paying attention to nonverbal signs and feelings you may be picking up from other people. In many places, discussions of relationships and money are rarely heard, but in other places, it may be off-limits to talk about whether a leader is qualified, about how much a work group gets done, about why someone got fired, or about how decisions are made.

Jamie Kerrigan is an expert at reading the air. As the front desk manager of a large luxury hotel, he knows which guests might be open to an expensive upgrade. He looks at what the guests are wearing (especially the shoes), the credit cards they use, whether it looks like a night for romance, if the guest is with someone they are trying to impress, and the communication between the guest and the person with them. If the guest looks like someone who can be easily persuaded or embarrassed into an upgrade, Jamie will swing into action and offer a luxury suite for an additional fee. It works. He and his team have one of the highest upgrade rates of any of the hotel chain's properties.

When I talked with Kosuke about holding off on his plans for the board meeting and instead reading the air first, he looked disappointed and dejected, but he listened. He went to the meeting in New York and didn't do much more than introduce himself, talk about the Japan division, and observe. In short, the primary thing he did was read the air.

It wasn't easy for him because he is an action-oriented guy. But when he came back to Japan, we met up again and he thanked me for my advice. He told me that he was glad he "had not dug [his] own grave" at his first board meeting. Yes, he was now a member of the board, but he had to figure out what that meant and what he could do.

"The board does nothing more than listen to the chairman's rants," he told me. "When a vote is taken, it is always unanimous in support of the chairman. There are country and regional sales reports, but there are never any questions from other board members, only critiques by the chairman followed by unanimous agreement by the board members. I'm glad I didn't present my strategy. I'll have to figure out another way to get my ideas across."

I told him how other-country CEOs I had worked with had to relearn how to read the air when they were appointed to a regional or global position. These executives were also chomping at the bit to put their ideas into play on a regional or global scale, but unless they read the air, they would never get that chance. They had to figure out what kind of influence they could have by first assessing the situation.

When Carlos Ghosn was appointed the CEO of Nissan, he was asked by the press what his strategy would be for turning around the then-ailing automaker. He told the reporters he had no plans to talk about yet. He wanted to find out what was going on first. He'd announce his turnaround strategy once he understood and could assess the company he now headed.

Ghosn spent months examining the strengths and weaknesses of the company, and he learned Nissan's culture. He looked at financial measures, marketing plans, concept cars, and the design pipeline. But he also had to read the air. He had to really understand the culture, especially those parts that are invisible. That's what he did before announcing his strategy and eventually leading the company to profitability. Ghosn became a well-respected leader because of the effort he made in understanding Japanese people, Japanese culture, and the Nissan culture.

Detectives such as Sherlock Holmes, Hercule Poirot, Columbo, and Miss Marple are experts at reading the air. My favorite is Adrian Monk, the main character in the American TV show *Monk*. Although Monk is best known for all of his phobias, he is able to pick up very important clues simply by walking around a crime scene. Sometimes Monk, played by actor Tony Shalhoub, holds up his hands as if framing a shot for a photograph while he develops an understanding of what happened based on his examination of the "air" surrounding a crime scene.

My clients are surprised when I talk with them about reading the air. Many non-Japanese people have never heard this expression. I tell them that anyone who wants to create the life at work they want, anyone who wants to be effective in what they do, has absolutely got to learn how to read the air.

I always read the air with every consulting client I have. The CEO or the human resources department may have given me their assessment as I begin a project, but I've got to understand the situation on my own. Clients call me when it is time for change, and I need to assess how ready the organization and the leader are for change.

There is a difference between what people say they want and what they are ready to do. People talk about wanting to change—"Everyone's ready," they say—but then do not take any steps in that direction. Our desire for change can outpace our ability to face the fear of changing.

As a professor, I watched and observed. I listened, I paid attention—to the students, the faculty, the relationships between people, and how other people reacted when a certain topic was brought up or when an administrator walked into the room. I followed the cry of advice in Arthur Miller's *Death of a Salesman*: "Attention must be paid."[2] I did what any good consultant would do. I observed and learned about the environment. That's how I could be most effective and eventually carve out a niche for myself.

I always paid close attention to any change in the mood of the classroom. If a typically outgoing student was suddenly quiet and withdrawn, I'd check with them at the end of class. The last time I did this I discovered the student was being troubled by nightmares and depression. We talked a bit more the next day and he started getting counseling. At the end of the term, he gave me a super-strong handshake and told me how much I had helped him. I didn't do much. I just paid attention and read the air.

Reading the air gets more complicated when you are in a foreign environment where the "air" is different. We bring our own perceptions and baggage with us wherever we go, and it's easy to misread the air in such an unfamiliar setting. In these cases, it may help to check out your reading of the air with colleagues from the local culture.

You can learn how to read the air anywhere if you are willing to be more patient in your approach to problem solving and recognize that you do not have all the answers. My training as a consultant and my experience in organizational change helped. But I think I got better at reading the air because I began to examine situations without preconceived assumptions and solutions.

How about you? Can you think of a situation recently where you read the air correctly before taking action? Have you jumped into the middle of a messy situation without really understanding it? What was the result? Reading the air is not limited to work situations. It's easy to misread the air in social situations, such as someone's romantic intentions. Think that person is interested in going out with you? Maybe, maybe not.

You can learn how to read the air by being more open; by observing, noticing, and listening without judgment; and without thinking you are always right.

In her book *Seven Days in the Art World*, Sarah Thornton describes what the best art auctioneers at places like Christie's and Sotheby's do when they conduct an auction. They look around the room, they make eye contact with current bidders, and they keep on talking until they can squeeze out another bid. They can almost feel if and when another bid will come.[3]

I also know about reading the air from my own mistakes and the mistakes I've seen others make. It's painful to watch. The person who fails to read the air looks foolish, and other people in the room scratch their heads or run the other way.

At a recent wine tasting event for about fifty people, a consultant who had written a book walked around with a copy of his newly published work and passed out his business cards to everyone who was there. He didn't stop to talk since he wanted to make connections and give a card to everyone. I doubt whether anyone will call him for his services or buy his book. He would have been better off having several conversations with just the people near him. He didn't see the looks on people's faces or their body language when he interrupted them for his pitch. He failed to understand that people go to these kinds of events to meet new people, drink some great wine, and eat good food. They do not go to be pitched to and annoyed by a consultant.

Reading the Air at Work

A university colleague of mine in Seoul is particularly effective in working with groups throughout Asia because she spends time understanding the process of change in countries where she works. She studies the culture, learns at least a few words in the language, and partners with a local consultant who is able to understand what is *not* talked about. The local consultant helps her understand the silences, interprets the meaning behind the words that people say, and knows the best way to configure the groups.

Sometimes in the rush to get things done, we forget to read the air or read it incorrectly. For a consulting project in China, I was hired to develop strategies for improving collaboration between a beverage maker's sales department and its marketing division. I made site visits to four sales offices, where everyone told me they worked seamlessly with the marketing division. "We'll go along with any changes that are forthcoming," I was told. I should have known better.

Actually, I did know better but wanted to believe what they told me. At that time, I didn't recognize that no one wanted to give an outsider a true picture of what was going on. I didn't recognize that when you hear almost identical stories from everyone, someone is usually not telling the truth. Once the company executives started implementing some changes, the differences between marketing and sales became apparent and the resistance to change was very high. We had to work hard to align those sales and marketing teams.

When I speak with groups about change, I tell them to beware of going too fast in the wrong direction or driving the bus without any passengers. Even when there is a green light to go ahead on a project, it does not mean full speed ahead. It means read the air and proceed with caution. A green light on a project is often more of a flashing green, a flashing yellow, or in some cases, a flashing red light: Stop and proceed with caution. Slow down and read the air.

Creating the kind of life you want at work does not mean you have to immediately change or adapt to the culture. Read the air first so you can decide what to do in that environment. Change can come later.

Reading the Air Gives You the Choice

And as you read the air, think about what you can do with your understanding of the organization.

Do you want to make some changes?

Do you want to create alliances with others with similar goals?

Do you want to fit in and follow the pack?

Do you want to add some value?

Where can you add the most value?

Where are the places where you can have the most influence?

Reading the air gives you a choice about what to do and how to do it.

During the time of Japan's economic "big bang" and the opening of its financial markets in 2001, I conducted research on the change in leadership skills needed at major financial institutions. One bank president told me his prime challenge was to go after new business opportunities while fending off competition from the large number of new financial institutions entering the Japanese market.

He realized those working under him would need a fresh set of skills to succeed in the changing environment, but he didn't rush in to change the way everyone worked. He knew everyone would have to be involved in the process.

Listening was the place to begin. Everyone needed to be included, and he started by canvassing the fifteen to twenty people in his department and listening to what each had to say about their work, their skills, their goals, and their dreams.

He observed the way people worked and identified the leaders in the group. He spoke with his staff about the increasingly competitive market and the need to cut costs. He chose not to hire a deputy, thus limiting the filtering of communication and the misperceptions that might result. Everybody recognized that things needed to be revamped, although they differed over how to get the job done. After talking with everyone and reading the air, he knew how to proceed. He told me he just "worked off people's menus." He talked with people, read the air, and then knew what to do. It was that simple.

Don't Read the Air at Your Peril

Those who don't read the air are not dumb. Typically they are intelligent, and their intelligence has usually served them well. But because they are smart, they think their intelligence is all they need to make the right moves. It is not.

I've met people who tell me they refuse to read the air. They tell me they want to do things their way, period. Unfortunately they don't understand what reading the air is about. They think that if they read the air, they have to do what others are doing. They confuse reading the air with fitting in and following along with everyone else. Reading the air is simply understanding the situation based on what you can't see.

What you do after you read the air is your choice. And you will have many choices based on what you now know. You could decide to fit in or you could decide to follow the Japanese proverb and "be a smart eagle who hides your claws" until a later time.

Choosing to fit in and do what everyone else does is common in Japan, where it's rare for someone to rock the boat. As the saying goes, "The nail that sticks out gets hammered down." But this choice might leave you feeling less than satisfied.

You can figure out what to do that won't kick up a lot of dust, something that will match the culture or nudge it a bit. You can go for the low-hanging fruit and do something that will be readily accepted. And you can do this under the radar so people don't notice what you are doing.

As a conference speaker, I always get to the location before my talk. I join the organizers for coffee or lunch and talk with people who will be in the audience. That's how I find out more about the group. I am amazed at the number of speakers who breeze in and breeze out, staying only for their own talk. Arriving early and staying late is how I can provide the most value. I find out what's on people's minds and supplement what I already know. I listen to what people say and notice what they don't say.

In our art gallery, we pay attention to everyone who walks in. We observe people before approaching them. Some people want to talk, some want to be quiet, some just want to use the toilet (yes, that's true too)—and we watch how they act when they enter the gallery. We've learned there are real differences in the art business between visitors who are art lovers and visitors who choose to purchase art.

We used to think that people who came in and looked at every piece of art and said, "I love it, that's beautiful, so interesting, etc.," would soon select some work to purchase. That's often not the case. They are most often art lovers who want to look at a lot of art and talk with us and the artist. They are most interested in seeing and learning and very rarely collect. They want to know about the artist and the techniques. They ask a lot of questions, pick up postcards and catalogs, and then go to the next gallery.

Collectors love art too, but they ask many fewer questions. They won't look at everything in the gallery but will zero in on the works that interest them. They never say, "Whoopee!" or "I love it!" when they see something they like. They keep their emotions more in check, but they can usually decide very quickly. They do not hesitate to buy. They say, "I like it. I'll take it." We need to read the air as we approach and spend time with the gallery visitors. The best salespeople in any business always read the air.

If you find the idea of reading the air baffling, you can give people an opportunity to make the air more visible with surveys, interviews, and suggestion boxes.

In one consulting project in Tokyo, we had trouble uncovering what was on people's minds. We posted large sheets of blank paper in the employee lounge where people could write down and draw the kind of changes they would like to see in the company.

We'd post daily questions such as: What are you thinking about today? What's on your mind? What's one change you'd like to see in this company? We worked from people's suggestions, just like the bank president I wrote about earlier.

Reading the Air Creates Value for Others

The young CEO of a start-up had complained to me that the people in his office were "so negative." When I asked him to explain, he told me they were not enthusiastic about the move to the new office he had designed. The week before, he had suddenly organized field trips to the new offices so people could see them. On that day, he was so excited that he could not work. He went ahead and interrupted everyone's work and took them all over to visit the new space.

People complained about not being able to get their work done and having to go with the CEO on his field trip. They were happy to be moving to beautiful new offices, but they didn't like being told to stop working. Morale suffered when he misread the air. "Why couldn't they get excited?" he asked me. "The new offices are so beautiful." No doubt the employees would have agreed if they had been able to visit on their own schedules.

The real plus about reading the air is that you can add value. You understand the organization. you know where the needs are, and you can act. When I started at Keio, several faculty members told me they hoped I would bring big changes to the faculty. Initially, I interpreted that to mean major changes in the way people taught or major changes in the curriculum. I proceeded cautiously, but even the smallest steps I made in those areas met resistance and, in some cases, backlash. I mistakenly accepted what people said as a marker for my path.

But once I could read the air, I realized I could provide the most value by teaching courses that others could not or did not want to teach. I developed and taught new courses like Creativity and Change, Artisanry in Japanese Business, Business Management in Asia, and Entrepreneurship. I also brought in some of my consulting clients as guest speakers since I had many contacts in the business community. These were contacts that the Japanese professors didn't have.

After fifteen years at Keio just quietly doing my work, one of my students told me a former dean spent more than half of his lecture talking about the positive influence I had on the curriculum at Keio. I had figured out what I could do to make a difference and add value. I didn't look for recognition from others, so I was a bit surprised when I heard what the former dean had said.

Reading the Air in Any Language

Not long ago, I sat down with a client who was ready to leave Japan after being disappointed that he could not develop a satisfying life working here. "It's the language," he told me. "I will never be able to understand Japanese people. How close can I get to Japanese people when I can't speak the language? I won't be able to develop any kind of fluency for several years." I listened, but I didn't agree. People who know the language can speak and understand words, but often they cannot read the air. In places like Japan and other Asian countries where so much is unsaid, reading the air may be more important than speaking the language.

I speak some Japanese, but only the most generous people would call me fluent. Not being fluent forces me to understand more of the intent of what people are saying and what people are not saying. This forces me to listen deeply to the meaning behind the words.

I've worked with many non-Japanese people who were fluent in Japanese but who could not understand Japanese people and develop meaningful relationships here. They focused on the words, not on the feelings, and not on what was unsaid. They often failed to understand the body language and the true meaning behind what people were saying.

In Bangkok recently, I met up with a friend who had moved to Thailand. He was fluent in Japanese and was now studying the Thai language. We decided to go to Somboon, a well-known seafood restaurant in the Silom section of Bangkok and a place I always visit when I am in Thailand. We hopped in a taxi and my friend gave detailed directions in Thai to where we wanted to go. The taxi driver could not understand my friend. And my friend could not see that the driver didn't understand and he just kept on talking, raising his voice with every word. "This driver must be new or dumb," my friend told me. We soon got lost.

I noticed the driver getting frustrated and confused. Finally, I just said, "Somboon Silom," and we changed course and soon reached our destination. It was a good example of how reading the air can save you frustration and points you in the direction you need to go. And, as in this case, reading the air can get you fed.

That was easy, but most situations we face at work are much tougher. It's a good thing. Tough is good. That's what we'll talk about in the next chapter.

CHAPTER FIVE

Tough Is Good

It was not an easy decision to leave my faculty position at Keio. I loved the job, the university, and the students. Keio had been my home for more than twenty years, but I felt like I had done everything I could do there. I had developed new courses, helped revise the curriculum, reached out to many faculty members, and taught thousands of students. I could have stayed on teaching part-time, as most professors do. But I wanted to do something else; I wanted to experience new challenges. I was afraid that boredom might set in, and that was the last thing I wanted.

I have seen what happens to people when they are bored and complacent and how damaging that can be. I wanted to take on some new tough challenges. I knew I wanted to write more, but I wasn't sure it would result in a book. I knew I wanted to have a career as a conference speaker, but I wasn't sure how to get that started. I knew I would also get more involved in the gallery that my partner, Hitoshi, and I had started seven years earlier. I had been preaching "tough is good" to my clients and students, and now it was my time to practice it with some new challenges.

Tough involves overcoming resistance to risk. I had many challenging times at Keio creating new courses and figuring out how to make a difference in a Japanese university, but I didn't realize what tough was until I got more involved in our gallery. Sales and cash flow were tough challenges that I never had to worry about as a professor.

Over the course of seven years trying to make that business a success, we got hit first with the collapse of Lehman Brothers in September 2008. One Lehman customer had ordered two very large paintings but could not complete the transaction once she lost her job. When Lehman crashed, a large number of our clients moved away from Japan.

Along with the Lehman shock, the global financial crisis resulted in even more of our clients getting laid off and leaving Tokyo. Those who stayed often took a salary cut and moved to smaller living spaces with less room for art.

When the devastating earthquake and tsunami hit Japan in March 2011, people stopped spending and fixed their attention on the earthquake zone. And even more people left. Tourists, another group of clients, also stopped coming in 2011. Many of our clients worked in financial services, and the cutbacks by banks in 2012 and the regionalization taking place because of globalization and cost-cutting drove even more of our customers to Singapore, New York, London, and Hong Kong.

Each time we faced a crisis that severely impacted our business, we had to come up with a new strategy.

The tough challenges forced us to rethink what we were doing and make significant changes. After these business shocks in the gallery, Hitoshi and I wondered how we could keep this business going. It seemed impossible to continue, but because we had our backs against the wall, we had to think of something in order to survive and ultimately succeed. Tough times forced us to use everything we knew.

We reached out to Japanese customers; we brought in lower-priced and smaller works. We sent out email blasts and postcards. We printed catalogs in English and Japanese. We worked with our artists to obtain an exclusive on some of their works, and we created a sales website. We ran events to educate younger collectors. We collaborated with wine companies, hotels, and restaurants and hosted events with wine, food, and art. We held a two-week exhibition at Mitsukoshi, Japan's top department store, in the very upscale Ginza district.

Tough is about ultimately believing more in growth than in fear and having the confidence to weather serious new challenges. It is about stretching to adapt to new situations and working in a way that was previously unfamiliar. When the going gets tough, you develop the strength to tune out your own anxieties and fears about change. Each tough punch the gallery took resulted in something good: We used our brains, we made some more sales, and we stayed alive.

Not too long ago, we returned early from a vacation to meet with a wealthy hedge fund manager in our gallery. We had corresponded with him over a period of six months and when he came to visit, he chose seven large, expensive works. This kind of sale was exactly what the gallery needed to bring us to a reasonable level of profitability.

But even after cutting our vacation short, sending scores of email images back and forth, and negotiating over price, the deal did not go through. The hedge fund manager did not buy a thing.

This hit us very hard. We really were ready to give up. After so much work and so much riding on this sale, I didn't think there was anything else we could do to keep the gallery afloat. We had tried so many different strategies. We really needed that sale. Now what? How could we attract clients who could afford some of our higher-priced works?

I wasn't sure what we could do to get those big sales. Sales of small items pay the telephone bill, but we needed the big sales to stay afloat. I wanted to stay true to my principles and not let this ruin my life, but it was a serious crisis. We weren't going to starve or get kicked out on the street, but this was a tough problem and we didn't know what to do.

Our idea stream was running dry at that point. And then, as I was making breakfast one morning, I thought of an idea that might attract the serious collectors. I felt so much joy when the idea came to me. It wasn't genius. It simply involved expanding our online sales to include more expensive items by partnering with art auction sites in New York. When you solve a tough problem, it can bring you joy. That was how I felt when we started implementing this strategy.

As I write this, I am not sure if this initiative will significantly boost our sales, but I was elated by coming up with the idea and tapping into the reservoir of my brain. The joy of it made me feel alive, relaxed, happy, confident, and competent. I got all of these positive, good benefits from a tough situation.

Tough really is good. This is what I always told my university students. I'd often begin a class by asking, "How was the assignment?" The answer was always a chorus of students saying the exact same thing: "Tough." I'd act surprised and tell them, "Tough is good. I'm doing you a favor. If it were too easy, you'd get lazy and complacent. A difficult assignment will prepare you for tough challenges in the future."

We'd all laugh, and then a few of them would yell out, a bit sarcastically, "Thank you *so much* for these tough assignments."

At work, you might be tempted to take on a task or project where you will surely succeed rather than one with greater challenges and no guarantee of success. You may be digging a small rut for yourself if coasting through the day becomes your norm. There are some real advantages to taking on what's tough. Enduring achievements are not forged by those who take the easy assignments. Challenging work keeps us engaged and feeling alive. As long as tough does not overwhelm you, it can drive you toward greater achievement and self-satisfaction.

How often do you hear people say they are bored with work? For me, it's much too often. Because I help people create the kind of lives they want at work, I hear people say, "I'm doing the same thing I did last year," "I'm treading water," or "I'm not learning anything new." People may be comfortable in terms of salary, security, and predictability, but they are so comfortable it is uncomfortable. If you're such a person, you may even be a bit jealous of others who are always doing something new and taking on big challenges.

Tough Boosts Your Skills

Tough is good because it teaches you. In one of my first consulting projects, which I wrote about earlier, I worked long hours, six or seven days a week. We'd joke that we were "working in the salt mines," but we learned a lot. The pressure to produce reports and write quickly was intense. Yet because of that pressure, we all developed writing skills that would serve us well in any job. I can usually write *x* number of pages without much prodding. I rarely get writer's block. In that job, there was no time for anything resembling writer's block.

A few years back, I consulted with Frank Reynolds, the CEO of a bank. He was driven to always be number one. Frank's father was a firefighter; his brother was in prison. His father put a lot of pressure on Frank to achieve.

Frank had been put down by some of the wealthier students at the elite high school and university he attended. To his credit, he took the toughest courses, excelled in his studies, and eventually earned the respect of the other students as well as his professors. He was accepted at a first-tier business school for an MBA and after graduation nabbed a job with one of the top banks in New York City. He competed with the brightest people in banking, knowing that all of those tough experiences would serve him well in the future.

Frank knew what I meant when I asked him, "What do you want to create today?" When he headed a small bank in Japan, he turned it into one of the largest asset management groups in the country. That was his dream. Everyone said it would be tough, and it was, but Frank was accustomed to tough. Tough for him had started at a very early age. Tough forced him to use more of his brain and more of his talents.

Frank couldn't do it alone, and he wanted others to know the good feeling that comes from tough. He wanted to see people develop and grow. He gave them tough challenges. The bank had been a sleepy operation, barely staying alive, but when Frank took over, everything changed.

The people I interviewed in the bank told me, "Frank believes in us, he pushes us. He teaches us to excel; he is a true leader; he gives us the confidence to achieve." Frank used his own experiences when he was younger to make sure others could also achieve something bigger than they had ever imagined. He gave them chances to succeed on tough assignments and rewarded them when they did. He shared the credit for the bank's success with them.

As I've said before, if you want more of a challenge, you don't necessarily have to change jobs. You may be able to get a greater challenge right where you are. You can talk with your boss or coworkers about taking on more difficult situations. You can design your own tough development program too. You can expand your own skill set with some tough challenges.

Gerhardt Schmidt, another client, headed a luxury sporting goods company in Korea. He felt his job had lost its challenge and its magic, but he didn't want to quit. We made a list of what he wanted to learn and another list of what the business needed in order to expand. We pinpointed those items that would add value to the company and those that would add value to Gerhardt. He then chose those items that appeared on both lists, and together we designed a series of challenges for him to try in order to revitalize his job. Among them: reaching out to international athletes for endorsements, starting joint ventures with fashion brands, and creating a flatter organization.

What about you? Are there tough tasks you could take on in your current job that can bring more of a challenge to your work? What actions can you take today?

Making the Best of Tough

Are you someone whose work is already tough? Some people I talk to say their work is tougher than they ever imagined. If this is you, what can you learn from your tough situation? And what is making it tough? Is it the amount of work? Is it your boss? Are there some actions you can take that will make the work not overwhelm you? Is there a way you can focus on work that will add value to your organization and be more interesting to you?

Try making a list of the most important tasks that will add value to your organization. Make a list of tasks that could be handed off to someone else—or that don't even need to be done.

Discuss what you want to do with your boss or your group. In a few organizations, such as Google and 3M, you can take time to work on any of your own projects that will challenge you and also benefit the organization. Wherever you work, you can integrate your own personal challenges into your job. For example, if you want to develop your skills in new product development, seek out new projects and add innovation to the projects and products you are working on now.

Tough helps you get closer to creating what you truly want. Think about those tough times as your teachers; learn from them. It's tempting to think that the road to success at work is a straight line of success after success, like going up an escalator. But more typically your work experiences will have their ups and downs, their good times and bad times. In the words of the Russian poet Yevgeny Yevtushenko, "Sorrow happens. Hardship happens. / The hell with it. Who never knew / the price of happiness will not be happy."[1]

As a professor, it would have been easy for me to teach the same courses in the same ways, every day, every year. Instead, I always threw out my lecture notes at the end of the semester. Boredom would have been like hell for me. I always reinvented my courses and developed new courses for future semesters. I did this because I wanted the work to be interesting for me and for the students. I needed the challenge. Was I making it tough on myself? Maybe. But it would have been worse for me to teach the same content every year. I would have been bored, and when the instructor is bored, the students will surely be bored as well.

If you are not engaged with your work, you'll likely stop paying attention and start making mistakes. When I see people making a lot of mistakes, I wonder if they might be bored. Correcting the mistakes they make may keep them engaged and challenged, but they and their organization suffer from those errors and oversights.

When a university colleague suddenly had to return home to Paris before the start of the semester to take care of an ailing parent, I had to find a substitute to teach his course. He told me, "Here are my notes. The person won't have to do much; the materials are all there." But the notes were *his* notes, for *his* classes, for *his* teaching style.

I expected that anyone who would teach the class would develop their own materials to fit the new class, the new students, and their own style. The person we hired did just that. He thanked us for the notes but told us he wouldn't be using them and would develop his own materials. The ostensibly easier way of using another instructor's notes did not suit him.

When I was a professor, I always encouraged new instructors to develop their own syllabi and was reluctant to share my own. It was not out of selfishness but in the interest of pushing new instructors to create theirs from scratch. I figured this tough approach would make the new instructors give more serious thought to the course, help them become better teachers, and would help them put their personal mark on their courses.

Tough Teaches You to Handle Challenges

Tough situations teach you to be more self-reliant. Give yourself tasks that stretch you, that challenge you. When faced with a tough task, you may fail, but you also could succeed. And it's always an opportunity to learn and grow. To put it simply, tough helps you develop.

Be wary of doing too much for the people you work with. When you do for others what they could do themselves, this may look like compassion and kindness. But in reality, you may be robbing them of the chance to develop. After all, how will they learn? What will they do when you are not there?

This approach has its roots in child development. Dr. Madeline Levine, author of *Teach Your Children Well*, wrote in the *New York Times* that in twenty-five years of private practice as a child psychologist, she observed that "the happiest, most successful children have parents who do not do for them what they are capable of doing, or almost capable of doing. . . . The central task of growing up is to develop a sense of self that is autonomous, confident, and generally in accord with reality."[2]

When we opened our art gallery, my partner and I didn't know anything about the business. It was tough. We had to learn so much in order to make the gallery a success. I had taught management and entrepreneurship courses at the university. I had been a consultant. I had been an art collector for more than thirty years. But in no way did all of this prepare me for running an art business.

We started out first in our home. We wrapped some prints mounted on cardboard with large sheets of Saran Wrap and hung them from the ceiling on fishing wire. I didn't think that framing or display was important. I didn't know about pricing, delivery, import taxes. We had a lot to learn. We made a lot of mistakes. It was very tough. But eventually, we learned how to run a gallery. In 2012, *Time* magazine called Tobin Ohashi Gallery "one of the top four places to see art in Tokyo."[3]

Tough Opens Up Opportunities

Tough can also lead to greater opportunities for you. Merle Okamoto, who, together with her brother, Ernest Higa, brought Domino's Pizza to Japan, first started out by selling frozen pizzas to small stores in Japan.

Frozen pizza in the 1960s was virtually unknown in the country. Most homes did not have an oven large enough for a frozen pizza. Nor did people have microwaves. Cheese consumption in Japan was and still is very low compared to other countries. And most Japanese freezers are tiny. What's more, Okamoto and Higa were just starting out in the food business. They certainly had it tough.

They had to teach customers how to make a pizza in a frying pan by crumpling up aluminum foil and putting it in the bottom of the pan and then putting the frozen pizza on top. The pizza would get heated in the frying pan and the cheese would melt.

They eventually succeeded in their pizza business, and their experience with frozen pizza enabled them to convince Domino's Pizza in the United States to give them the rights for Domino's Pizza in Japan.[4]

Culture Clashes Are Tough

When I first came to Japan and started teaching at Keio University, the customs of a Japanese university were utterly new to me. The meetings were conducted entirely in Japanese and would go on for four or five hours. Every professor had a chance to talk and voice his or her opinion. Since everyone was so polite, no one would ever say, "Enough," if the discussion went on too long.

Students would sometimes show up on the last day of the semester to take the final exam and expect to pass even though they had never attended a single class. There were piles of paperwork to request even something as routine as a video to show in class.

I had to find my own way, and it was not so easy. Thankfully, there were people who had my back. The dean and associate dean were my big supporters, as were several senior faculty members. They wanted change in the curriculum but would not drive it themselves. They saw me as an instrument of that change.

I paid attention to what was going on. I tried to read the air and understand what was possible. I had to figure out for myself how I could add the most value. As I wrote earlier, I developed elective courses that I thought would most benefit the university. As a foreigner, I could offer courses no one else could. I could reach out to other departments, and I could be a catalyst for bringing people together.

I broke a lot of rules and had a few head-on collisions with other faculty, but that didn't get me very much. Those clashes succeeded only in driving people away. I learned a less confrontational, more Japanese way of working. Once I stopped fighting, I had more energy to teach and write. I didn't have people critiquing me, getting in my way. My work became much easier. People consulted me, treated me better, and respected me. And I respected them.

Tough Brings Out Your Best and Leaves the Rest

My tough times have been small compared to the tough times that artists face. Artists are willing to make huge sacrifices in support of their art. The term "starving artist" is all too often true. They scrimp and save and work part-time jobs in order to have enough money for materials so they can create art. They put their work out there for everyone to see and critique. They hear people say things like, "What is it? . . . I don't understand it. . . . It's ugly. . . . I could do that."

Gakushi Yamamoto, a sculptor who works with our gallery, has his MFA, but he still works as an assistant to one of his former professors in order to have access to a studio. He works part-time creating models for sculptures for Disneyland, and he also does hard physical work helping out at a moving company.

Sometimes after working on one of his sculptures for months or even years, he has to melt it down because it didn't sell. There's no storage room for the sculpture in his studio space and he has to use the raw materials to create another work. I have seen him stay up all night to make a handcrafted box so we can ship a sculpture overseas. I have never heard him complain or make an excuse. "This is part of an artist's job," he tells me.

Creating a great life you want at work means being like the Japanese tumbling doll, the *daruma*. The *daruma* is red and round with a face on the front. Most are about the size of your clenched fist. When you buy a *daruma* or get one as a gift, you make a wish and then color in one eye. When the wish comes true, you color in the other eye. The *daruma* is weighted on the bottom so it always rolls back up, no matter how hard you push. It encourages people to keep on bouncing back so their dream can come true.

You have to work at creating something you want for yourself. If a situation is tough, you bounce back, you keep at it. There are times when you will need to reach out to others for help. There are times when it's not possible to bounce back quickly, but when you keep on going in the direction of your dreams, you can persevere. That's the lesson of the *daruma*.

Enjoying and Embracing Tough

Think of tough situations as puzzles to be solved, puzzles that will help you use more of your brain and more of your creativity. One fashion client I worked with liked to give people challenging, real-world problems in a job interview, such as, "What kind of celebration would you plan for the fortieth anniversary of the button-down shirt?"

He got to see how the applicants' minds worked. He got to see how quickly they could generate ideas. The applicants got a chance to be creative and have some fun (although they were certainly a bit nervous too).

When you have a tough job or a task, don't hide behind the excuse of being a beginner or being only temporary. When an understudy has a chance to take on the part of an actress who is unable to perform, she will give it her best. In some cases, the understudy's performance will surpass that of the lead. She doesn't say, "I'm just the understudy." She embraces the role as her own and in some cases it really does become hers.

If you are in a temporary position, a volunteer, an intern, or just working part-time, avoid saying, "I am just a part-time worker," or, "I'm not getting paid enough to do that." Instead, remember that the part-time or temporary job can turn into a permanent one. Consider yourself the understudy who has a chance to learn and show what she can do. I have clients who are now in challenging, high-paying jobs because of their excellent track records in their volunteer work—the most low paying of all.

One young Japanese venture capitalist I met recently in Hong Kong was not sure venture capital was the career he wanted. He was on the lowest rung of his organizational ladder, but he still had access to millions of dollars in venture funds and could refer people to his colleagues who made the decisions about funding. When I met up with him for a drink, he told me he didn't feel very comfortable in the role, and he was worried that it was hampering his effectiveness.

I couldn't understand what he meant until he told me he was telling the funding applicants, "You know so much more than me," "I am just a beginner here," "Thank you for teaching me." This is a very common way for Japanese people to speak. They are very modest about their skills and accomplishments. As we talked, however, this young man recognized that he needed to embrace the position and had to stop demeaning himself. The situation was tough, but he was giving all of his power away and making himself inconsequential. If this was the career he wanted, he needed to fully embrace it.

Shinobu Namae is the chef at the Michelin-starred restaurant L'Effervescence in Tokyo. The *Wall Street*

Journal wrote an article about the magic Namae can do with a turnip.[5] Yes, a turnip. He spent a couple of years working at the Fat Duck in London, a restaurant considered by some to be the best in the world.

Tokyo is considered one of the premier places for food on the planet, and it wasn't easy for Namae to succeed in the crowded fine-dining world of the city. But Namae did—through hard work, talent, and by challenging himself again and again. He never stops developing new items to add to his menu. One of my favorite dishes is a salad with thirty-five vegetables. Yes, thirty-five. He is always trying out different food combinations. He works like a scientist as he maps out the chemical formulas for some of his combinations.

When you've finished your meal at L'Effervescence, Namae will come around to your table to say hello, thank you for coming, and find out how you liked your meal. The first time I visited, I asked him if it was tough running a restaurant that is a destination for global foodies. He told me simply, "It's tough and it's fun. I'm always thinking of new ingredients and combinations all the time. I even dream about what may be possible with food. I wouldn't do this if I didn't love it."

Too Tough?

Some tasks are not just tough; they are impossible. If I were asked to develop a marketing plan for a new interior design studio, that would be a stretch. But I could do it. Not the same for developing a fund-raising plan for an opera company. I don't know very much about fund-raising or opera and I don't have a list of potential donors. This is not an assignment I would take. It would be *too tough*.

There are also times in your career where you may not want any more tough situations. You may want to take it easier, take a break, or do something else. You may want to say, "I'm satisfied. It's enough. I can handle tough but I don't want to."

You may want to spend more time focused on your personal life and your family. You may be at a stage in your life where you've done everything you wanted to do, or you have everything you need. You may want to coast at work (if you can) because you are taking care of elderly parents or three dogs. Or you may just be fed up.

That's what happened to one of my clients, the head of a chemicals company division that was bought out by another American firm. Two years later, it was sold to a Chinese firm. The next year, it was sold back to the American firm. As the CEO, she had to merge her company with the acquiring company three different times. She had to adapt to new ownership; she had to lay off employees; she had to deal with the press and stockholders. She certainly acquired a valuable set of skills during those tough times, but it all proved too much.

After the firm was reacquired by the American company, she stayed on for another six months and then she left. She knew she could handle tough situations, but it was time for her to create something different for herself. She walked away, not out of fear, but out of a desire to realize a more personal dream and create a different life for herself.

Like Attracts Like

If you are someone who can handle tough situations, you will attract similar people. When you complain, you will attract other complainers. Take on tougher situations and you will notice that you will attract friends who like challenges. This happened to one client who left a pharmaceutical company to join a boutique mergers-and-acquisitions firm specializing in pharmaceutical companies. Once he took on this tough challenge, new friends came into his life. He didn't have to look for them. They found him. One of his new friends runs a nonprofit that helps young fashion designers. Another is a real estate investor. Another runs a company that plans unique corporate events.

As he took on more challenges himself, he didn't want to be with people who were not challenging themselves. He wanted to be with the best. "There are small things that I didn't expect," he told me, "but I found a wonderful group of friends, a magnificent apartment, a great gym, and an excellent internist." Because he was tackling tough situations and working so hard, he attracted the best people to him.

Don't be surprised if your friends who don't like a challenge or complain a lot drift away from you as you embrace tough. Some may change because of your positive influence, but you may have to get rid of the jerks in your life. We'll talk about those jerks in chapter seven. But next, we'll examine the importance of courage in creating the life you want at work.

CHAPTER SIX

Courage Matters

C reating a great life at work means following your own path. It means not worrying about what other people think. And it means showing courage. That's one characteristic shared by everyone who has the life they want at work.

What is courage? I define it as the ability to do something even when it frightens you. Courage means facing uncertainty and making a decision in accord with your beliefs.

Let's start with an example from my recent experience as a professor in Japan. My teaching assistant, Hiroaki Yamane, had worked with me for two years, taken my classes for three years, and also helped out with the gallery. We worked closely together, so I was a bit surprised when he sent me an email telling me he would not be able to work with me during his final semester.

When we met up later that week, he told me he was leaving school to take an internship in Chicago.

He said he might not have enough credits to graduate if he left early, but he was going to leave just the same. He'd miss all his classes for the second term.

He saw the internship as a once-in-a-lifetime opportunity, and he didn't want to miss that chance. The internship was with a small company that special-ized in creating better user interfaces for websites for big companies such as Nike and Coca-Cola. The company was best known for working on the visual design of the 2008 Obama presidential campaign.

He wasn't asking me for my opinion. He had made up his mind and was going to take the internship, even if it meant not graduating. I was tempted to tell him to stay around and graduate. That would be the safe thing to do. But if I said that to him, it would be more about my own fear and it wouldn't be true to my own mes-sage. Instead, I listened to how excited he was about the internship, congratulated him, and wished him the best.

Hiroaki was truly showing courage. He might have had some fear, but that didn't matter to him. He had made his decision and was going to take the internship in the United States. Courage doesn't mean the absence of fear; it means being able to take action even when you feel fear.

There was no shortage of people telling him not to go. Other professors insisted he was doing some-thing very dumb. They told him he should stay around and finish school first. Hiroaki listened to them but didn't waver. He showed courage, left school to take the internship, and spent the next few months in Chicago rather than in classes at the university.

He returned to Japan briefly right before final exams and found he was a couple of credits short for graduation. But he didn't give up. He persuaded two professors to let him complete the assignments and take the tests in the classes he had missed. He quickly wrote a few papers so he could earn enough credits, and he *did* graduate. He got some very valuable experience as well. The internship had not prevented him from earning his degree. His courage paid off.

He stayed on another two years as a full-time employee with the same company and worked on projects that took him to London, Paris, and the U.S. West Coast. While he was in Chicago, he was offered a job that paid twice as much, but he didn't take it, recognizing that he wouldn't be learning much there and also that he didn't want to work for a big company. He then took a job with a small start-up in California doing cutting-edge, large-scale data mining. He took the job not because of the salary, but because it gave him a chance to use what he knew and, most important, learn new skills. Now he's in Portland, Oregon, working with AKQA, an innovative agency that creates cutting-edge projects for Nike and other big clients. His courage really paid off and his career went in a direction it might never have gone had he stayed around for that final semester in school.

We don't hear the word *courage* used much in business in Japan. You may hear similar words—*risk*, *guts*, or *taking chances*—but not *courage*. That's because in Japan adherence to the norm is so strong. Courage may mean going against your boss, your parents, big companies, or older people, all of whom are supposed to be deserving of your respect and often your fear. Showing courage might result in being isolated, becoming some kind of pariah in a group or in your family.

What we do hear a lot about in Japan is the lack of risk taking. And it's very true. Twenty years of a stagnating economy combined with a desire for job security and the high value placed on the norms of hierarchy have made many Japanese young people risk averse.

Many don't ever want to leave Japan. A *New York Times* article cited a Japanese Ministry of Education and Science report showing the number of Japanese students studying abroad had "declined 11 percent to 67,000 in 2008, compared to 2007." The number was down 20 percent from "its peak in 2004, and that downward trajectory has continued since 2008."[1] Education overseas and fluency in English might give them a leg up in employment with a global company, but many Japanese just don't want to leave. When Harvard president Drew Gilpin Faust visited Japan in 2012, she met with students and educators who told her that "Japanese young people are inward looking, preferring the comfort of home to venturing overseas."[2]

This aversion to risk is not the entire story. Young people like Hiroaki Yamane are taking a more entrepreneurial and a more individual path. Their numbers are still small compared to those in the United States, but they are starting their own companies, working in Silicon Valley, and connecting with other entrepreneurial types worldwide. There are start-up dating salons helping to match would-be collaborators. Many of my former students are in this group. Instead of joining Japanese trading companies and manufacturers, they are starting their own companies right out of school. They live in houses they share with other young entrepreneurs.

It's as if there are two Japans, one becoming more conservative, another becoming more adventurous. In some of Japan's high-rise office buildings, you see these groups converge. There are start-ups on some floors and divisions of traditional companies on others. The people wearing shorts at the start-ups cross paths with the corporate people in suits when they all take their coffee at the Starbucks on the first floor, but they rarely interact.

I use the word *courage* precisely because it's rarely heard in Japan. There's a high priority on being part of the group and following the pack. The stereotype of risk-averse Japan is so strong that it is easy to hide behind this terminology and blame it on the culture: Japanese people don't like risk. I use the word *courage* because it puts the responsibility where it belongs: on the individual and no one else. Emphasizing the responsibility of the individual makes it hard to hide behind cultural norms.

Courage was the most important message I aimed to get across to my students. I encouraged the students to have the courage to dream, to change, to be who they are, to speak up, to follow their own path, and to take the next step.

The courses I taught had names in the university catalog such as "Leading Global Organizations," "Business Strategy," "Communication," and "Change and Creativity," but courage was the underlying message. Innovation, change, and leadership all require courage, and I encouraged the students to do what they never dreamed possible, including starting their own businesses. In a time when most Japanese students were staying put and not venturing overseas, a large percentage of my students opted to study abroad for at least one year.

Courage has been a big part of my own consulting and speaking practice. Executives need the courage to change, to have tough conversations with their bosses and their boards, or to announce and implement a new strategy. When one client was appointed to head a global marketing effort for his company's major product line, the role was a big stretch for him. He needed to find the courage to lead the team. In his words, he was now in the big leagues. The thought of leading people who were considered stars in his company scared the hell out of him, but it didn't stop him.

Courage also means ignoring the "noise" you hear from others. People may tell you you're crazy. They will criticize you, tell you to be cautious, or fill your head with fear. They will tell you you're not ready. They will encourage you to stay put and avoid making big changes, especially when the pressure to conform is so strong.

Recognize that some of those people are genuinely concerned about you, while others are simply giving voice to their own fears. They might even be jealous of what you are doing. They wish they could do it. My usual comment when I hear such criticisms is to just say, "Thank you." Listen to them, but you do not have to follow their suggestions. As Shakespeare wrote in *Hamlet*, "Give every man thy ear, but few thy voice."[3]

It takes courage to break away from the pack, but the good news is it's something you can do for yourself. Unlike playing tennis, showing courage doesn't require a partner. You don't need to get permission from anyone. You don't need the approval of others.

Dealing with Fear

Summoning your courage means dealing with your fears. But first you must know your fears to overcome them. Do you know what is holding you back?

Is it fear of failure?

Fear of your parents?

Fear of rejection?

Fear of what other people think?

Fear of success?

In the words of author Marianne Williamson, "Our deepest fear is not that we are inadequate. Our deepest fear is that we are powerful beyond measure."[4] When you're considering something new or a step in a new direction, ask yourself these questions:

Why not?

What could I lose?

What could I possibly gain?

What gets in the way of me taking that step?

Acknowledge your fear. And recognize that somehow, you have to put it aside. Ask yourself as many questions as needed until you can identify your fear. What are you afraid of? What could happen? You'll lose money? Be embarrassed? Your mother will be upset? You'll lose your car?

Don't get angry at your fear. Make peace with it. Don't let it consume you. Just keep it on the side and shake hands with it. Your fear is still there, but it's no longer controlling you. Dealing with your fear gives you power and courage.

Write down everything you are fearful about on a piece of paper and then throw it away in a wastebasket, or "flush your fear" down the toilet. Symbolically, you can throw your fear away. This really does work, although you might be skeptical. It has worked for thousands of my students and clients.

But you're not done with fear yet. You need to understand why you have that fear. The reasons why you are fearful may come to you right away, but it could take a very long time—especially if it's a memory you have long ago repressed.

Here's one example from my own life: giving a speech. Now I earn most of my income making speeches, but for a long time in my life I was afraid to do so. Afraid is an understatement. I was petrified. I would shake and panic when I had to give a speech in high school or college. Often I skipped class on days I was supposed to give a speech. I hoped the professor would forget or I would try to arrange to give the talk privately in the professor's office.

There were some speeches I simply could not avoid, such as defending my dissertation, and to prepare for those, I would write the word *fear* on a piece of paper and then throw the paper in the toilet. This really worked for me then and it worked for me after grad school, as a consultant and professor. Symbolically, I had gotten rid of it. I cleared my head and was not overcome by my fear.

But as I gave more speeches, I kept on trying to understand why I had that fear. I wanted to understand where my fear came from. In my case, it took years before I found the answer. Its roots were way back in my childhood. Beginning in elementary school, I was always good at giving a speech or a talk. I was the kid in school who got the leading role in the school plays. I was the kid who read the announcements on the public address system. I was the one who excelled at show-and-tell.

So why was I filled with so much fear now after having been successful at giving speeches when I was young? I eventually recognized that although giving a speech earned me big applause and the respect of my friends and teachers, I was often ridiculed at home. My parents would attend show-and-tell at school, they'd come to the school plays, they'd be there when I gave talks at PTA events, and they'd even hear me give talks at the religious school I attended.

On the way home in the car, my parents would tell me about all the mistakes I had made. They'd tell me I should be embarrassed because of the terrible job I did. They'd tell me how ashamed they were of me. I'd hear a lengthy critique from both parents about what I did wrong. I'd hear about a stumble I made when I started or a word I mispronounced. Once I got home, they'd yell at me about any of the talk's points that were not logical.

I had completely repressed my memories of this damaging criticism, which continued from childhood all the way through high school. By the time I got to college, I just gave up and fear took over. My parents were no longer there, but their critiques were alive in my head. I didn't even know why I was afraid; I just stopped giving speeches.

Why should I give a talk and subject myself to the abuse I imagined I would be hit with? At the time, I wasn't conscious of what was stopping me. I didn't recognize what was holding me back. I just knew I was scared out of my mind.

I spent many years trying to figure out where my fear came from. I finally recognized these influences from my past when I was well into my thirties. This became a turning point. The next step was looking at my current situation more realistically. I was no longer living at home, and my parents were no longer there to criticize my speeches. Most people said good things after I gave a talk. No one ever nitpicked the missteps I made. I had been stuck in a past that no longer existed. In my own mind, I had been re-creating that past, but now I began to smash it and clear it from my mind. It took years.

The question "What do I want to create today?" helped me diagnose my fear. As I thought about what I wanted to create and my dreams, I knew I had to come to terms with the fear I felt. Figuring out where your fear comes from will require a great deal of reflection and self-examination. This is not an easy job for any of us. The source of your fear may be something you have buried deeply. Was there a traumatic experience that made you steer away from any kind of risk? Were there messages you received as a child that made this particular behavior so uncomfortable for you?

Without courage, you may lose once-in-a-lifetime chances. A few years after graduate school, I was contacted by people assisting management scholar Peter Drucker about working with him. It was a chance to start something new. It was a chance to work with the world-renowned author, educator, and "father of modern management."

At the time of the call, I hesitated. I was afraid to put myself in the big leagues of management training and consulting because I was afraid I might not be good enough. I was afraid I'd get stinging criticism. I was afraid I would fail. Or was I afraid I might succeed? Was I afraid I'd be too good at it and would have to give up the old image of myself and my low self-esteem? In any case, I said no and I never got another invitation from Drucker or his associates. I missed that chance because of fear.

I didn't even think of that as a lost opportunity. In a way I was relieved because I didn't want to put myself in a self-imposed hell where I would always be thinking I was not good enough. Maybe you know that feeling. You get offered something most people think would be great, but it causes you no end of anxiety.

Over the years, I began to realize I did have talents that were worthwhile. The feedback came from my students, my clients, and my colleagues. I began to realize that if I wanted my dreams to come true and go beyond what I was doing, I'd have to put my fear aside.

Dreams Drive Courage

Your passion for your dream can help you find your courage. If you have a dream and the passion—a fire inside you to make something happen, to do something you absolutely have to do—then the courage will come and the fear will subside.

The fear becomes small when the dream is big. When your dream is strong, it becomes easier to show your courage. It may not even seem like courage. It will seem like something you *have* to do. Want to have more courage? Want to put aside your fear? Try focusing less on your fear and more on making your dream stronger.

Kei Hamada, one of my former students, was a frequent visitor to our gallery from the time we started up. He loved art. "Art was my best subject in school," he told me. He had gone to work for a major Japanese electronics company where his father was a high-level executive. But it wasn't a perfect fit. He worked hard to succeed, but his heart wasn't in it. Yet he didn't want to quit because he thought it would be embarrassing for his father, and he wasn't sure what he wanted to do.

He spent every weekend surfing and also started drawing and painting again. He even put on a couple of exhibitions. He bought some art from our gallery. I introduced him to our artists.

He came by the gallery one day and asked me to recommend some schools for an MBA. I was surprised, and somewhat jokingly asked him why an MBA, why not an MFA? He gave me the answer I've heard from so many: "An MBA will help me succeed." An MBA would be the magic bullet he needed, he thought.

I suggested he consider whether this was something he really wanted. "An MBA is not for everyone," I told him. An MBA helps people who really love business and want a career in business, but I didn't get the feeling that was what he wanted. I asked him what kind of life he wanted. He described a life by the beach in Kamakura, Japan, where he could run a small art studio and gallery and surf. It didn't sound like he needed an MBA for that. He worried what his friends and family would say. He worried about how he would earn a living.

We talked a few more times. Kei told me his teachers in elementary and high school saw his artistic talent. He began thinking about going to art school and yes, getting an MFA, or at least continuing his education in art. He started looking at art schools, thinking about an MFA or a BFA.

I introduced him to Masako Kamiya, one of our gallery's artists, who teaches at Montserrat College of Art in Beverly, Massachusetts. After meeting with Masako, he visited the school, applied, and was accepted. He quit his job in Tokyo, headed to Italy for a special painting program, then moved to the United States and enrolled at Montserrat. Here's part of an email I got from him:

> I am feeling more relaxed doing my artwork now. I feel like I come up with creative ideas and improve my skills and mentality every day. It is the pure enjoyment of doing art and there are so many motivations. This is something probably you cannot experience when you are working at an office, or once you have grown up. I feel like I am now going in the right direction. In addition, I am meeting all professional artists who make their living as artists, and am visiting their studios. I am doing well, and motivated every day.

He's happier than ever before. His dreams helped him to push aside his fears.

Every day we have a chance to show our courage. We could have that uncomfortable conversation with a colleague who is bothering us. We could call the venture capitalist we met at a friend's party and pitch him a couple of business ideas. We could talk to our boss about the project we really would love to do. We could tell our parents we won't be making the sixteen-hour flight to come home for the holidays. We could eat that raw oyster.

But something stops us. We may say to ourselves, "I'm too busy," or, "The timing is wrong," or, "I tried that before." There is no end to the excuses we can come up with. But it's really the lack of courage that stops us. We become accustomed to certain patterns in our lives and a way of looking at ourselves and we lack the courage to change.

This lack of courage creates its own kind of hell. In the words of writer and spiritual healer Stephen Levine, "Safety is the most unsafe spiritual path you can take. Safety keeps you numb and dead. People are caught by surprise when it comes time to die. They have allowed themselves to live so little."[5]

Many consultants like to tell the story of the baby elephant that gets chained up to a pole at birth and gets so comfortable in that position that even when the chain is unlocked, the elephant doesn't try to escape. Consultants use that story to illustrate how we can become too comfortable and too afraid to take risks. I also like a story I modified from a parable, a tale about a criminal named Mario.

Mario had been arrested for petty crimes and sent to a local prison. He was a likable and sociable guy, and he made a lot of friends among the other prisoners. He also got along well with the guards. Even the warden, who coincidentally was from the same area of Sicily as Mario, befriended him. The warden would often stop by Mario's prison cell and they'd share memories of their hometown. The warden liked Mario so much that one day he told Mario he would help him escape from the prison that evening. He left the keys to Mario's cell and to the prison gate under Mario's pillow. He explained how Mario could use the keys to escape and no one would know.

The next day, the warden dropped by and expected to see Mario's cell empty. Instead, Mario was still there. He never used the keys and handed them back to the warden. He told the warden, "Thank you, but I can't leave. I'm comfortable here." He did not want to leave for an uncertain life. He lacked the courage to use the keys. He had grown comfortable in prison, where everything was predictable.

Mario's situation is not unique. In fact, you have the keys to change your situation every day. You have the keys to do something new. Now. Complacency, lack of courage, and fear keep us where we are.

You can start by taking small steps toward the life you want. Talk to a friend in another department about a transfer or a project. Invite a new colleague to join you for lunch. Ask the waiter to take the burned lamb chop back to the kitchen and serve you the rare one you requested.

Small steps lead to larger steps. Courage builds up over time, especially when your courage has positive results. Eleanor Roosevelt, the longest-serving first lady of the United States, wrote:

Courage is more exhilarating than fear and in the long run it is easier. We do not have to become heroes overnight. Just a step at a time, meeting each thing that comes up, seeing it is not as dreadful as it appeared, discovering we have the strength to stare it down.[6]

While success can help you develop courage, failure can do the same. You get rejected by someone you want to date or by a company you want to join, and instead of giving up, you develop the resolve to try again or explore other possibilities in earnest.

In Japan, it's not unusual for people rejected by a top university to spend another year or two in an exam preparatory school where they study six hours a day so they can try again to pass the entrance tests. I taught students who had failed Keio's entrance exam three times, and still they came back to take it a fourth time, at last succeeding. Robert Pirsig, the author of *Zen and the Art of Motorcycle Maintenance*, took four years to complete his book and received 121 rejection letters. While some might have given up after one or two rejections, Pirsig persevered and the book was finally published and went on to sell more than five million copies.[7]

Once you find your courage, think about what you're going to do or what you're going to say. Write down what you want to do with your courage. Will you talk with your boss or your partner? Will you move toward your dreams? Will you start planning a transfer to a position in another country? Practice what you want to say in order to put that courage to good use.

Some people find it easier to show their courage when they're angry. But anger may throw you off balance and push others away. They will respond to your anger and not your request or your announcement. Make it easy on yourself. Consider what you can do or say that will not be stressful to you or others but will still achieve the desired result.

I like to watch Barack Obama at his press conferences. When a reporter asks a hostile question, Obama doesn't ever lose his cool. He doesn't get angry or emotional when he answers, but he often takes a risk in answering the questions. Sometimes he puts the reporter on notice that the question is inappropriate or draws a line in the sand stating his position very clearly.

When using your courage, first choose a strategy that has very little emotional cost to you. If necessary, you can use more of your courage and power later. Don't use it all at once. It took you a while to get it.

And consider how you will respond to others who criticize you. You may feel compelled to respond when you are confronted by people seeking to do damage to you or treat you shabbily. You need to respond— not through direct confrontation, which plays into their hands, but with smart tactics that disarm your maligner.

Consider, for example, rude or inconsiderate treatment from your boss or colleagues. Here are three responses you could use in dealing with a bully at work. Say them in a normal conversational tone and you'll soon find the bully changing his target.

1. Say, "Huh?" Say it loud and clear, as if you didn't hear or understand what the bully said. Another version of this is saying, "I don't understand what you mean."

2. Say, "That's an inappropriate (or unacceptable) comment." Put the bully on notice that what he or she said will not be tolerated.

3. Say, "That's not helpful." It doesn't matter that the person never meant to be helpful. This response catches them by surprise. A longer version of the same response goes something like this: "I'm not sure why you would think that sort of comment is helpful."

Let others know what you don't like and the negative impact it has on you. "I don't like when you munch on chips in my office. The crumbs get all over the floor."

Don't forget to communicate the change you want: "I'd like you to stop."

Be careful about relying on others to encourage you to take action and show your courage. Some friends, colleagues, or even your boss may say they'll support you all the way, but instead they might really be encouraging you to take action they fear taking themselves. They're comfortable pushing you out onto the plank. They'll cheer you on, but disappear when it comes time to jump. You might even be set up to fail, taking the fall for others.

Have you been in situations where others pushed you to speak up? Maybe you wondered why they didn't say anything themselves. They might have been more than willing to have you take the hit for saying something while they silently watched.

I was lucky to learn this lesson early on. In graduate school, I signed up for a course in social psychology, and the professor assigned more than ten heavy texts to read during the term. During a fifteen-minute break from class, all of the students complained to each other about the amount of work. The other students, most of whom were studying clinical psychology, encouraged me to "say something." In my naïveté I listened to their advice but didn't tell them they should speak up as well. Here was a chance, I thought, to show my courage and leadership.

I went back into the classroom after the break and voiced what we all felt: "It's a lot of work for one course." The professor looked surprised and asked if anyone else felt the same way. Not a single one of my classmates who complained during the break raised their hand. In fact, a few lashed out at me. They told me I shouldn't be speaking up since I was from another department, not psychology. I ended up dropping the course, and I learned something about groups and courage in the process.

You may find that other people's stories give you courage. I like to read inspiring tales of professional athletes. As a boy, I enjoyed stories about Bob Cousy of the Boston Celtics and Ted Williams and Jim Piersall of the Boston Red Sox. Piersall's book *Fear Strikes Out* chronicles his triumph over bipolar disorder. I devour stories of Ichiro Suzuki, Hideo Nomo, and Hideki Matsui, all of whom left hugely successful careers in Japanese baseball to begin new careers in professional baseball in the United States. And they triumphed in the United States as well.

I'm always looking for inspiring stories that I can use in my talks. There are many similar true tales of professors, writers, and, of course, entrepreneurs. Sadaharu Aoki, now one of the best-known *pattisiers* in France and Japan, at first didn't even know a word of

French when he headed to Paris in order to learn the art of pastry. Now his creations are famous—and delicious. Choose stories based on your interests.

These stories may encourage you to take the needed steps to break away from the pack. But don't be so caught up in other people's stories that you hesitate to act. It is your own story that you must create.

The artwork we show in the gallery is a source of inspiration for many people. Visitors tell us that the art makes them feel relaxed, happier, and motivated to take action. When they take the artwork to their homes or offices, the paintings continue to inspire them.

Although I too get inspiration from the paintings we have in our gallery, I find courage in the stories of the artists themselves. It takes courage to become an artist: The rest of the world does not necessarily support you in your decision. In fact, most people will tell you to do something else. They'll tell you how hard your life will be, how you'll starve, or how your work is not good enough.

Others will cite statistics showing the dreadfully low incomes of artists, musicians, and actors. They might even tell you to study accounting so you'll have something to fall back on. If a young person says, "I want to be a doctor/a banker/a lawyer," people will say, "That's wonderful." It's not the same for those who want to be artists. The young people who want to be artists must take a big step and follow their hearts—and that takes courage.

Artists' need for courage does not stop with their choice of career. They cannot be afraid of making mistakes. They must always push themselves to create something new, something fresh. That means going in new directions, even when so many others are heading a different way. The title of this book comes from Ida Bagus Putu Purwa, one of our artists from Bali. He told a newspaper reporter that he goes into the studio every day and asks himself, "What will I create today?"[8]

And when the artist changes, the people who liked what the artist did previously will ask, "Why did you change? I loved your other stuff." But the artist does not go back. He or she must again defy convention and have the courage to move ahead. In creating art, artists follow their dreams. The courage of artists encourages and inspires us to recognize and realize our deepest, most important drives and dreams.

Ryota Aoki, one of the ceramicists we represent, works fourteen hours a day creating ceramic vessels, cups, and dishes. He is always creating something new. He will test more than a thousand glazes to come up with the exact color he wants. And after all that, he is subject to the vagaries of the kiln, which might easily destroy his work or result in a very different hue than what he expected. But he never stops.

Another artist we work with, Jun Ogata, creates canvases that are inspired by Japanese gardens and seem to "say Japan" to many people. He primes the canvas, then paints it black or white, then adds a silver or gold coat, then adds another color. When all of the coats have been applied, he faces the canvas and in one second he takes a cloth or a brush and removes some of the paint. In this moment, he can create a beautiful artwork or destroy what he has done. That kind of gamble takes courage.

How much courage will it take for you to move toward the life you want at work? Where will you find that courage? Can you leave all of the excuses behind? Can you put the fear aside? When will be the right time for you?

You are already moving toward creating the kind of life you want at work, but to get there sooner rather than later, you'll have to clear away the people who are holding you back. You'll have to get rid of the jerks. In the next chapter we'll talk about those jerks and how to find the best people for you.

CHAPTER SEVEN

Get Rid of the Jerks

Surround yourself with the best people. That's what I say to every client I've had and to every class I've taught. You need to surround yourself with the best collaborators, colleagues, suppliers, bankers, customers, bosses, and friends. Even the best dentist.

Sometimes without us knowing it, the people around us keep us stuck. They keep us from achieving what is possible. They tell us, "I don't think you should take that job/join that gym/marry that guy." Of course they may have our best interests in mind, but it's also possible they are worried about you leaving them or surpassing them.

The best people are those who support you in what you are doing. They help you succeed. They get you involved in challenging projects. They are happy to see you progress. When you see them or work with them, you feel energized, not drained. They value you, not tolerate you. When you choose the best people, you'll be able to do more of what you want to do and you'll have a greater impact in the work you do. You'll welcome the connection you feel with others. You'll feel more powerful, not beaten down or second-guessed.

Take Jeff Char, a serial entrepreneur who runs Venture Generation, a community for early-stage ventures in Tokyo. Jeff trained as a lawyer and joined a top-tier law firm, but that was not for him. He then helped many people, including me, set up new businesses and spent years as a venture capitalist. But Jeff had a dream. He wanted to do more to stimulate the growth of entrepreneurship in Japan, and he wanted to be surrounded by the best people, people with similar dreams.

He found a suitable space in downtown Tokyo, spoke with almost a hundred entrepreneurs, and then selected a group of start-up companies to take a desk in Venture Generation's large space.

The people in these start-up companies at Venture Generation work on making their dreams come true. They talk things over with Jeff and each other. Jeff invites successful entrepreneurs in to give talks over pizza lunches. He has surrounded himself with people he wants to be with.

The work you do matters, but *who* you work with is critical to having a great life at work. Jeff didn't just choose the *companies* for Venture Generation. He chose the *people*. He wanted active people who are creating something. He chose people who will benefit from his expertise and from being in a space with other start-ups. He surrounded himself with people who will add value to the other companies, and he chose people he and others can learn from.

What about you? Who are the people who surround you? Do they support you? Encourage you? How can you surround yourself with the best people?

You could, of course, create an entirely new situation or enterprise like Jeff did, but that may not be something you want to do right now. Instead, you can take a series of steps to find the best people for you in the work you do. And you don't necessarily have to change jobs.

The First Step: Knowing Who the Jerks Are

Do you ever feel as if you are surrounded by the wrong friends and people at work? Your friends and your colleagues are your mirror. Could these people be jerks? Jerks are those people who regularly waste your time, the ones who don't value you, the ones who may abuse you, and the ones you want to avoid. They hold you back. Your body gets tense when you see them. They are the ones who always keep you waiting. They are the ones who drain your energy. When you see them, you may have to take a deep breath just to have the strength to deal with them.

I have had them in my life. Too many of them. Consulting clients who always pushed for a price cut and were never satisfied with the work I had done for them. Faculty colleagues who spent more time spreading rumors than doing research. Gossipers who would suck me into conversations berating others. I often didn't know they were jerks because it was so comfortable being with them. I just figured everyone was like that. It took me a while to learn otherwise.

Do you know who the jerks are in your life? It's not so easy to tell because your judgment might be clouded. People don't come right up and say to you, "I'm a jerk," or, "I'm bad for you." We usually find people whose views of the world are the same as ours. We may have chosen to be with them because they share some of our own fears and anxieties. Their views about who we *are* also reflect the way we *see ourselves*. But as we change and see ourselves more positively, we are less willing to be with people who do not value us. We no longer will tolerate others' bad behavior.

Some distance, a bit of a break, or a complete separation from the past can help us in getting some clarity. After the change, you will be able to see your situation more clearly.

If you have even a sneaking suspicion that some of your relationships, business and personal, are less than the best, take a careful look at them from some distance. Ask yourself whether you would choose to be with these people if they were just coming into your life now.

Working with the No Jerks Rule

Once you have a clearer idea of who the jerks are, it's time to start enforcing the No Jerks Rule. You don't need any jerks in your life. Getting rid of them sounds like a great idea, but maybe you're wondering how you do it, especially if you are not the boss or if you are working in a large company.

No matter where you work you can get rid of most jerks. Start by spending a lot less time with them.

If there are people you consider jerks in your department or organization, do what you can to minimize the amount of time you spend with them, or get rid of them. You may not have the power to kick them out of your organization, but you can make some moves so you don't have to work with them or be around them. Say no to certain projects and make it your policy to work with people you want to work with. You won't always be able to pull this off, but you can at least decrease your interaction with the jerks.

Some efforts at getting rid of them will be easy. If there's a jerk in the human resources department, talk to someone else who can understand your requests immediately and will process them. Seek out the competent people in every department who are easier to work with. Bypass or get rid of the person who is a hassle to deal with. If your in-house support services are a pain in the butt, use outside services when you can. They might even be cheaper, and you will find contractors who are happy to have your business.

When the jerks ask you to go to lunch or out for a drink after work, just politely say no and eat at your desk or go out with other people. You might eat alone for a while, but it will beat spending time with people you don't want to be with.

These kinds of changes are not always easy, especially in Japan, where harmony and relationships are so important. In Japan, people worry that making a change will ruin the relationship or be a hassle for others in accounting, the IT department, the delivery service, or whatever. But if you can change, the sooner you do so, the better.

I know from personal experience that it is hard to get rid of the jerks. Our gallery suffered for too long with an accounting firm that did not add any value and, in fact, wasted our time. I had a long relationship with the senior partner, so I was reluctant to make the switch. A junior accountant would come to our offices and check over every single one of our receipts and question us about the smallest expenditures. He sat in the corner of the gallery, spent hours checking the receipts and sales, and interrupted us when we were with customers. Even a government tax examiner would have added more value and asked fewer questions.

Finally, we got rid of this accountant and now have a great one who is also a business partner. He helps us, gives advice, and wants to help us grow our business. And he's less expensive than the accountant we fired.

When you think about the jerks, ask yourself, "Why do I tolerate this behavior from this person?" or, "Why am I spending time with this person?" Too often, you might stick with someone just because you're used to each other. It's only when you make a change that you realize how much better your life is. You might think that it's better to try to change the jerk. Let's be serious. They will change when you change. Maybe you can change them, but don't make that your goal. Instead, think of yourself first. Think about how much easier life will be without them.

When my friend Noriko changed jobs, she got a whole new group of friends. In her old job, she used to complain with her colleagues about how boring the work was and how hard it was to find someone to date. But in her new job, most of the other people in the office were married, and they liked the work they did and the work she did. Within a year, Noriko got married and almost completely drifted away from her friends at her old job.

You don't necessarily have to *confront* the jerks at work once you are ready to say goodbye. Just let them gently slide away and out of your life. You will likely have a transition period where you will be alone. Have confidence that there are new people out there for you.

It might be tough if it's your boss who is the jerk. You could get a transfer or wait until he or she takes another job. But you could also stake out a project for yourself and develop a reporting strategy you both can live with. For example, if your supervisor is micromanaging you, you could propose a plan for morning or weekly meetings where you could talk about progress. That's the system I worked out with one client and her boss who was calling her with questions and comments at all hours of the night. In this way, she headed off the ongoing reviews and interruptions.

The economist John Maynard Keynes wrote, "The difficulty lies, not in the new ideas, but in escaping from old ones."[1] He was referring to ideas, but the same applies to people too. Leaving the old friends is the hardest part. Finding new ones is easier.

What about those people you just don't like or ones you don't want to run into? You could go out of your way to avoid them, of course. That's the easiest way. But that gives them too much power. Why should your behavior be changed because of them? One technique I use when I see people I'd rather not see is to act like I'm seeing them or meeting them for the first time. In this way, I leave my own prior baggage out of the equation. I say hello and that's it.

When nothing seems to work with the jerks and you have to keep them in your life, you can make certain topics off-limits. When I was in my twenties, my parents would frequently ask me when I was getting married, but at the time I had no intention of getting married. Invariably, we would argue. I wanted to still see my parents, so we agreed to make the topic off-limits. You too can make those hot-button issues not open for discussion with certain people.

What if the jerk is your biggest client? You may not choose to get rid of them right away because you need the income stream, but you can spend less time with them while you find better clients. Be careful about the new clients you take on. You have to be sure not to partner with another jerk, like those people who go from one bad marriage to the next.

Many years ago, Dan Domancich, my friend and business adviser, told me, "Bad clients drive out good clients." When you have a client who is draining your energy and taking an inordinate amount of your time, it leaves you less energy and time for other clients. New clients could be wary of working with you if they recognize that another one of your clients is a bad actor—a jerk.

The same is true for employees and friends. Bad employees drive out the best employees. If you are having trouble attracting the best people in your organization, it may be because there are some jerks there that others do not want to work with. The best people want to work with the best.

Could You Be Creating Jerks?

The toughest questions to answer may be the ones you have to ask yourself: Did you choose to surround yourself with jerks? Are you in some way responsible for someone being a jerk? Could you have created this pattern of behavior and bad treatment? Have you been too passive? Or have you been a pest? Jerks aren't always jerks to everyone. You could have played a role in the bad treatment you're receiving. Even jerks treat some people well. Why not you?

Begin by examining your own behavior. Consider how safe you feel with the jerks. You may have turned others into jerks or contributed to making the relationship an unsatisfactory one. There might be one guy in your work group you always ignore who then starts doing things such as harshly criticizing your work in order to attract your attention. Or you might turn someone into a jerk by gossiping about them or never acknowledging their contributions. A perfectly good worker can become an irritant to you because of the way *you* work with *them*.

I had a consulting project last year with a company's VP of human resources who complained that his direct reports were not "team players." As I spoke to more people in the organization, however, it was clear that it was the VP who was dividing the team by holding secret one-to-one meetings where he bad-mouthed other team members. He was the one dividing the team.

In the past, I ran workshops on how to deal with difficult people. One of the big eye-openers for me and the workshop participants was how *we ourselves* do things that turn others into difficult people. If you bother the tech rep unnecessarily at all hours of the evening, for example, her demeanor may soon change from friendly to hostile. She's now difficult.

Are You Caught in the Drama?

The Karpman Drama Triangle, a psychological and social model of human interaction developed by Stephen Karpman in 1968, illustrates the three main positions in unhealthy relationships. Individuals play the role of aggressor, rescuer, or victim. Staying in those roles gives people the illusion of power and keeps them stuck.[2]

A boss may yell (aggressor) at a customer service representative (victim) for not doing his job well, and another colleague (rescuer) comes along and consoles the customer service rep and tells him everything will be okay.

But things may not turn out okay at all. The boss will yell some more. The customer service rep will become accustomed to the yelling. In a surprising switch, the customer service rep might turn into the aggressor not against the boss, but against the helpful colleague, who then takes on the role of the victim. The customer service rep might yell at the colleague, "You're bothering me, leave me alone!"

The roles incorporate learned patterns that bond people together in unhealthy ways. They are symbiotic, destructive behaviors that affect all members of the group. We may not even know we are in this unhealthy pattern because it has become the norm for us.

The best place to be on this triangle is nowhere. If you recognize yourself playing one of these roles, choose a new way of interacting with your colleagues. Get off the triangle. Your relationships at work will improve. People will treat you better. Most jerks will stop being jerks. You can even stay where you are without changing jobs. Your work situation will be much improved because you have changed.

Getting Ready for the Best People

You've heard people say, "Why do I always attract the losers?" The answer may be that they are not ready for the winners.

Before I met my partner in 1990, I really didn't think I could find someone who would value me, and I often accepted less than the best. I was not ready to let someone good into my life. There were many good people around, but I wasn't ready for them. I was more attracted to people who did not respect me.

If anyone liked me and really valued me, I would find some reason to reject them and devalue them. How could they like me? I wondered. And I would get upset with them—not ostensibly for liking me, but for some small thing I didn't like in them. I wasn't aware of the real reason I didn't like them. I figured they were nuts for liking me, so I came up with false issues. In fact, the biggest jerk in these situations was me for having a less-than-robust self-image and failing to recognize I was driving good people away.

As I've said before, you may worry that with the jerks gone you will be alone and by yourself forever.

You might even worry you'll die a lonely death with no one at your bedside. This is fear rearing its ugly head again.

It is more likely that just the opposite will happen once the jerks are gone. You'll be open to meeting new people, you'll have more energy, and you'll attract others to you—for the simple reason that you rid yourself of those who were hampering your life.

Finding the Best People

I admire people who have figured out who they want in their lives and make a point of surrounding themselves with the best people. They won't tolerate dysfunctional behavior. Once you are ready for the best people, they will find you. Think of yourself as a quality luxury brand that will attract people who appreciate your skill, your way of working, and the contributions you are making. You won't have to hunt for the best people. You'll find them by reputation, theirs and yours.

Will Smith is best known as an actor, but his life and words are often very inspiring to people. He's frequently quoted as saying this about finding new people in your life: "Don't chase people. Be yourself. Do your own thing and work hard. The right people—the ones who really belong in your life—will come to you. And stay."[3]

You can attract the best people in your organization by the good work you do. When your reputation is a good one, the best will seek you out. As you develop a reputation for getting things done well, others who also add value or are innovative will want to work with you.

When I first started as a faculty member at Keio University, I focused on my writing and on being a great teacher. I began teaching something unique, something different from what the other faculty members were doing. I also wanted to bring people together. I hosted events for faculty members and businesspeople. I introduced my students to my consulting clients. I encouraged students to have a wide perspective and big dreams. Consequently, the students who were attracted to my classes were the ones who wanted to be challenged.

As other students and professors learned of my work, they recommended some of their best students for my classes. I didn't have to promote what I was doing. I simply let the results speak for themselves. And the best people came.

Takeshi Yukawa, an associate dean, sought me out. He did what he could to support me and the work I was doing. He introduced me to other faculty members he thought would be good colleagues. He invited me to his home to meet his family and talked about his life, hopes, and dreams. He arranged dinners at historical buildings to help me learn about Japan. He invited other people on the faculty whom he wanted me to meet. He arranged grants for my students to take field trips. He made sure I got additional research funds and invitations to special events. He arranged for me to teach in graduate school and shepherded me though the necessary approval process.

I was fortunate Yukawa and I connected early in my career at Keio. I did not seek this person out.

He found me—and I admit I was lucky he did. You will find the right people when you focus on doing your work well.

Think about where you work now. You can check around and find out who does the good work. Most likely you already know them by reputation. Even in the most chaotic work situations, there are those individuals who live sanely, are getting things done, and are respected by others. You'll hear about them. Often the same names keep coming up. You'll see them in action in committees and group settings, and possibly have a chance to work with them. Make it your mission to find them and know them.

In one consulting project, I interviewed more than a hundred managers in a very large organization. When I asked them who they went to for advice, the same name came up again and again. When I interviewed this person, I too was impressed. In a giant bureaucracy, he knew which rules to follow, which rules to ignore. He knew how to get things done. He was practical and optimistic. He cared about the people who worked for him, and he cared for the organization.

Who are the people like that in your organization? Find them. Don't ask for anything from them. Consider whether these are the people you want to be with. You'll be on their radar screens and there may be opportunities to collaborate with them. Learn from them. They'll introduce you to others as well.

People who get things done hang out with other people who get things done. The people who *talk about* getting things done hang out with those who do nothing more than talk and complain. As a professor, I always avoided the faculty room wherever I taught.

That is the place where the energy is dead and only complaining is alive and well.

When choosing colleagues, notice what they talk about. Are they excited about the work they are doing? Do they talk about the past, the future, the present? Do they have dreams?

What makes work *great* is the human connection. What makes work *fun* is the human connection. How about you? If you were putting a classified ad in the newspaper for people you want to work with, what characteristics would you ask for?

You can find the right people anywhere, and some of the places you find them may surprise you. The most creative people won't necessarily be in the design department, and the most humanistic people won't necessarily be in the human resources department. In our gallery, many designers drop by and tell me the work they do is more routine than creative. The human resources people I meet in some companies talk more about numbers than about people.

Tokyo, with thirteen million people, is the world's largest city. Still, some of my single friends tell me they can't find anyone to date. I ask them if they're ready. I ask them if they are attracting the wrong kind of people. I ask them what kind of person they would like to meet. I tell them the story of my high school and university friend Peter Feeney, who worked as a VISTA volunteer and writer and traveled the world, living a very free life. No matter where Peter lived, he found a wonderful partner to be with.

Peter was good-looking, but more than that, he was a good person to be with, accepting of everyone, nonjudgmental, able to open his heart, generous with his time, and interested in others. When he lived as a VISTA volunteer in a rural Vermont town of fifty-four people, he had a wonderful girlfriend to share his time with. It was the same wherever he went. Be the kind of person others want to be with. Enjoy your life, do the best work you can, and the best people will find you.

The Added Value of Good People

There are those times when others will see something special in us we don't see in ourselves, something we don't even know exists. They even can see through the clouds of our own anxieties.

The feedback we get from teachers, consultants, classmates, and friends can be very helpful. I am forever thankful to my high school English teacher Alice Teed, who praised my writing, singled me out to read my essays to the class, and chose me to give the morning announcements to the whole school. These are small things, but they made a difference to me when I was young. I still remember her classes and the way she drove us all to a high level of achievement.

When I first met my friend Tom Pedersen, my consulting was primarily management training focused on midlevel managers in Japanese companies. I went to companies such as NEC, Hitachi, and Toshiba and taught middle managers about *how things worked in America*. In the beginning, it was interesting. I didn't know very much about Japan and I learned as I taught, but after about six months, I got bored.

Some of the managers who came to the training were just filling the seats and looking for a rest. Others were engineers who were told to learn about management. The people on the client side were also very strict about sticking to the curriculum. I was not able to interject my own expertise and ideas. I wanted to do something else, but I wasn't sure what. I stopped doing these training programs—I got rid of what wasn't working for me and I was ready for something else.

When I told my friend Tom about my dissatisfaction with the training I had been doing, he told me, "You shouldn't be working with midlevel managers anyway—you should be working with CEOs." He could see talent in me that I couldn't see myself.

What? I couldn't believe what he was saying. How could I possibly succeed with CEOs? But Tom felt CEOs would be a better match for me. I was scared out of my mind, but it turns out he was right.

I interviewed CEOs of foreign companies in Asia to find out what challenges they were facing. After I completed the interviews and wrote up my research for a popular business magazine, I started getting calls from CEOs who were looking for a coach and a consultant. My entire consulting practice began to focus on chief executives.

I needed someone who could see the potential in me. Tom Pedersen was that person. He saw something in me I didn't see in myself and gave me a push to go after it. Years later, I was able to repay the favor when Tom was looking for a job with a bank and I encouraged him to call the person I knew who was doing the hiring.

Good friends often see you in a better light than you see yourself. Sometimes we need the push teachers, friends, or our partners can give us. The mark of a great teacher, coach, boss, or friend is that they can see something in you that you don't see in yourself and illuminate that something for you. Jerks don't ever do that.

No Jerks Allowed

There are organizations where jerks can flourish, organizations where jerks can hide, and organizations where no jerks are allowed. Like soil that is good for some plants and not good for others, some companies have cultures that nourish and reward jerks, and other companies have cultures that get rid of the jerks almost immediately.

Think about where you work. Can jerks rise to the top? Is there a very clear message from top leadership about inappropriate behavior? Thankfully, there are many organizations where jerks are not tolerated. Company leadership lets them know in no uncertain terms that their behavior is unacceptable. In many surveys over the years, these organizations have been rated among the best places to work.

Other organizations suffer harassment or employee discrimination lawsuits almost weekly. These are the places headhunters know to avoid. Some organizations like to refer to themselves as "thankless cultures." They expect a high level of performance, and if you reach that level, well, it's nothing special. It's what they expected.

I admire the high expectations these organizations set, but I do not applaud their approach. In these companies, the only time you get attention is when you *don't* do a good job. That kind of culture lets some bullies and jerks flourish—bullies who continue to browbeat their employees to work harder, often without helping them acquire the skills needed to do the job.

One key to your organization's toleration of jerks is the level of thankfulness. In Japan, thankfulness is a pervasive aspect of the culture. You'll hear an announcement on the train platforms thanking you for taking the train. The staff in the gym will thank you for taking their aerobic classes and for swimming in the pool.

When I started teaching at a Keio, other faculty members would come up to me in the hall and thank me for teaching the students. Often at the end of each class, the students would thank me and applaud.

Non-Japanese people will sometimes say all this thankfulness is "superficial" or "insincere." There are certainly times when it is, but I think the opposite is more often the case. It is usually heartfelt and signals that people notice the contribution you are making. And anyone who does not express thankfulness quickly stands out.

Think about where you work. Is "thank you" something you hear often or rarely? Are people able to express their humanity and kindness? Do people hide their humanity because they want to appear more businesslike or because they are afraid that showing their humanity will hurt their advancement?

About a year ago, I consulted with a big bank about its low morale. Everyone who worked there had experienced turbulence—mergers, acquisitions, layoffs, and trouble with regulators. I headed a team of people who conducted an employee survey interviewing clients and suppliers as well as employees. After we analyzed the results and presented our findings to the CEO, he asked me, "Where can I start? What can I do today to make a difference?"

I stepped away from the data and told him that "thank you" would be a perfect place to begin. I suggested he thank people for their hard work, thank people for putting up with all the changes, start taking teams out to lunch, and show appreciation for people's performance, for their flexibility. "It will really make a difference," I told him.

And that's what he did. When I met with several employees a few months later, there was a noticeable difference in the way they talked about the company and the CEO. They told me, "He appreciates what I do here; he wrote me a nice note when I got promoted; he invites us to lunch. He *thanks* us for our opinions." This was a remarkable change in a very short time. Simple acts of kindness can make a major positive shift in the corporate culture and can ensure that the best people stay.

Want people to appreciate what you do? Show that you appreciate them. And when appreciation is pervasive in your work environment, the behavior of jerks will be unacceptable. Some of those jerks may even change; others will simply leave.

And when the jerks leave your life and your organization, you'll not only say goodbye, you'll recognize what you were able to learn from dealing with them. Every situation offers an opportunity to learn—which is what we'll talk about in the next chapter.

CHAPTER EIGHT

Learn Forever

The 1997 Asian financial crisis almost crippled the companies of William Heinecke, the CEO of the Minor Corporation, one of the largest hospitality companies in Asia. Tourism and spending plummeted as the Thai currency tanked and consumer spending disappeared. Heinecke didn't panic. He didn't fire his executives. Instead, he told them to go out and learn something new. It didn't have to be accounting, marketing, or anything business-related. He told them to study whatever they wanted. He sent them away to learn.

Several executives learned how to pilot a plane, others learned how to scuba dive or speak a different language. Heinecke learned how to drive a race car. And when they returned to work, all of them had new knowledge and new perspectives that ultimately benefited the business as it expanded throughout Asia and the Middle East.

In the same way that we need to exercise our muscles and hearts to stay in good shape, we need to exercise our minds to keep us challenged and engaged with our work. Learning benefits us with greater memory retention, patience, and confidence. And learning helps us have the life we want at work. Feeling stuck? Looking for a new challenge? Ask yourself again, "What do I want to create today?" Learning will help you move in the direction you want.

I like it when I see global executives using their time on the plane to learn about the countries they will visit. When people recognize some words in the local language and develop an understanding of specific cultures, they can connect with people by listening and developing an understanding of the local customs and business practices. They recognize that the more they learn about each country, the better it will be for their own businesses.

Learning enables us to open our eyes wider. Learning helps us dream bigger. We begin to think in new ways. The options available to us increase. And I don't mean only traditional learning such as going to university or grad school or studying for a professional degree. Such formal education can certainly make your dreams bigger, but it also can reduce your options. I've had many lawyer and doctor clients who desperately wanted to do something else but did not want to make a switch because of all the money they had invested in their educations. There's a lot we can learn on our own, on the job, while we travel, and while we pursue our hobbies.

New Challenges Keep Us Engaged

Traditional Japanese companies do not expect people to have specialized knowledge when they hire them. They train people their way. They might hire young people who majored in marketing and train them as accountants. Trading companies such as Mitsubishi and Sumitomo will hire Spanish literature majors and send them to France. It's sink or swim, and the individual has to learn quickly. Often, because the learning curve is so steep the first year, employees are continually engaged and bond with each other throughout the grueling pace of the training experience.

Some global organizations dispatch individuals to a different country every two or three years to ensure the learning and the challenge are always there. It's rare for hotel general managers to stay in a hotel's top job for more than three years. The major hotel chains, especially in Asia, where there is explosive growth, frequently move managers around and assign them to different properties. The general manager must learn a new system and culture, and brings a new perspective to the hotel. Everyone at the hotel keeps learning.

I like to think of learning on the job as a type of compensation. The next time you have a big challenge, remember that you are getting paid while you learn. You spent money for the degree you earned in a formal educational program, but learning at work is often more valuable than the education you paid for. And it's better than free. You are getting paid to do it.

What you can learn on any job is usually clear right from the start. But there are times when the learning is not so apparent and it's you who needs to identify what you are learning or could be learning. After I quit my job with Chapman University and the U.S. military and decided to stay in Japan, I taught English at an English conversation school. My job was to talk with students in English and help them with vocabulary and grammar. I didn't know very much about teaching English, so I developed those skills. But the biggest benefit was what I was able to learn about Japan and Japanese culture.

Teaching English was very personal. I could ask questions and students would answer honestly. "What did you do last weekend?" we'd start. "I studied for entrance exams." "What are entrance exams?" "Don't you know Japanese people spend years preparing for university entrance exams?" And the conversation would continue. Students would talk with me about their bosses, their families, their difficulties meeting someone to date. When I asked about hobbies, some students told me theirs was Japanese archery or ikebana. Since so much of my time in Asia had been on military bases, I didn't know very much about Japanese people and culture. Teaching English gave me a chance to learn much more than teaching skills.

Continuous learning requires effort. You need to make your learning a priority. Throwing out my teaching notes at the end of every semester forced me to learn something new every session. If your work is not challenging, is there still something you can learn there? How about learning about yourself and other people, as we have discussed in previous chapters?

Trouble with your boss? A client driving you nuts? You can learn how to handle challenging situations such as these. You can learn which situations you like best and which clients and people you like to deal with—and those you'd rather not.

When clients tell me they've learned everything they can in a job, I suggest they make sure they learn as much as they can about themselves before they quit. Otherwise, they are likely to make similar mistakes in the next job.

One Facebook friend, not a client, sends me a new note every other year with his Christmas card telling me he has just landed a new job as director of finance for a high-tech company. "This is a great job with a great company," he writes. But I've heard this at least three times before. He usually lasts about six months, has a fight with the boss or some of the internal clients, spends a year looking for a new job, and then the cycle repeats.

I consider confronting him and asking what he learned in the last job about himself, about getting along with his boss and others, and what he'll do differently the next time around. But I don't say anything. He'll write later and tell me that he got "ambushed again," that there was a global reorganization, or this time the boss was envious of him. He has not, so far, been willing to look at his own role in all of his troubles at work. That's what we must do to avoid making the same mistakes again and again.

Every situation gives us an opportunity to learn about ourselves. Getting fired or laid off is one of the best times to learn and change, but it's painful to think of the role we may have played in losing that job. It's easier to think it's the boss's fault or the result of a reorganization. Truthfully, in most cases job loss does not happen because of one incident or one reason. It's likely there are many contributing factors.

We can learn a great deal trying to understand what happened. A career coach or outplacement counselor can help in the process. But we have to be cautious about thinking we automatically know the reason. This blinds us to exploring other possibilities. In fact, to get the most learning out of any such situation, we have to act as if we don't know anything and are coming in fresh, open to exploring all possibilities.

The Problems with Knowing Too Much

Just about every day when I'm in Tokyo, I head to my gym for swimming class. I can swim fairly well, but I want to improve. It feels good to use my body and head, plus it's fun. The strokes have changed since the time I learned them in elementary school. I like learning the new methods and enjoy the physical exercise. I also like the advice the instructor gives. When a fifty-year-old man showed up for the first time in class, he told the instructor that he just wanted to brush up since he was already a good swimmer. He said had been on the swim team in high school.

The instructor told him, "Forget everything you know. All the strokes have changed." He was right. So much had changed it would be better to start with a clean slate. In that class, we start from the beginning with breathing and the positioning of our arms and hands. What anyone remembers from before doesn't help, and it can get in the way. You may have learned to "cup" your hands when you do the crawl, but now the most efficient way to swim is to keep your hands flat with the thumb extended.

I am amazed when people tell me they are an expert on Japan or, in fact, an expert on anything. Nobel Prize winners always talk about how much they still have to learn. Yet ordinary people describe themselves as experts and gurus on LinkedIn. There is so much to learn, and what is known in the world is always expanding. It's a big plus when you don't seem to be an expert. It means you're open to learning new things.

I'd often tell my students to "act dumb," act like they were seeing something for the first time. That's how they could learn the most. When they analyzed case studies and came up with answers too quickly, they'd risk not fully understanding the situation and considering all of the possible options. That's one of the dangers of acting like you know too much.

Another danger is that people will stop telling you anything. I've had clients who acted as if they had all of the answers and had nothing more to learn. But it worked against them. The people who worked for them stopped telling them anything. The employees learned to keep their mouths shut.

Some companies rush to release products in Japan without understanding the local culture and ignore their local staff. One chocolate company insisted on pink boxes for their Valentine's Day chocolate promotion, and the results were disastrous. Others had warned the new CEO that pink boxes on Valentine's Day wouldn't work since on that day in Japan women give chocolates to men. The CEO didn't listen. He believed he knew the chocolate business and the Japanese market. Plus, he loved the pink packaging. His staff gave up trying to dissuade him. The pink boxes didn't work. The chocolates didn't sell.

Knowing too much can also stifle conversation. "What a beautiful rose," you tell your friend. He tells you the Latin name, where it came from, on and on. The next time you see him with tulips, you don't mention a thing. You don't want another botany lesson.

Often it is the smartest people who don't feel like they need to learn. Harvard professor Chris Argyris, in his classic *Harvard Business Review* article "Teaching Smart People to Learn," wrote that "even though success in the marketplace increasingly depends on learning," more people just don't know how to do it. This is especially true for "the well-educated, high-commitment professionals who occupy key leadership positions in the modern corporation."[1]

Being consumed by your own self-perceived brilliance is in reality a major learning disability, one that gets in the way of critical self-reflection but also of creativity and innovation. At its worst, it can result in harm to individuals and organizations. Smart people too often act as if they have things figured out and know all the answers. It's always a pleasure for me to work with CEOs who want to learn as well as lead. When the CEO is open to learning, others make a greater contribution and learn as well.

Being flexible and open enables you to keep on learning. You have a plan but are willing and ready to change the plan because the situation changes. As a professor, I would usually prepare my classes in advance. But there were days when I would think I needed to challenge myself and the students more. I'd think it might be better to create something more fun or with more involvement. On my way to work, I'd see something or read something in the newspaper and develop a much more interesting lesson on the spot. Those classes were some of my best.

In a program I ran on team building in the Philippines for Japanese, Malaysian, Chinese, and Filipino engineers, I was told everyone spoke fluent English, but when I arrived the first morning to begin the training, the learning director told me that the Chinese and Japanese engineers could only read English, not speak it.

I didn't freak out. I very quickly figured out how to do the program using a combination of sign language and short phrases by grouping the engineers according to their different levels of English proficiency. It worked. For me, it was a chance to learn and develop new skills. The program participants learned new ways of working and communicating with each other.

When There Is No Learning

Recently, I met up with a former student who had been working for a government agency since graduating two years earlier. He told me he was "doing only routine work," basically filling out forms and scheduling deliveries. For him, it just couldn't get any more routine than that. He was paid well and he had job security, but there was no opportunity to do anything else for the next three years, his scheduled time for training.

The repetition was killing his motivation and sapping his energy. I asked him if there was any way he could make the job more challenging, if there were things he could learn there. It's always best to find a challenge where you are before making the life-changing decision to leave. He said he'd been told the job wouldn't change much. He said there really wasn't anything else for him to learn there, and I believed him. He decided to leave a few months later.

During a sabbatical from my university position, I was a visiting professor at Thailand's Chulalongkorn University, where I taught courses on organizational change, business management in Asia, and business strategy. It was interesting to go to another country and teach students from Thailand and more than twenty other countries who attended through exchange programs. I liked teaching there, I learned about Thai culture, and I had to create and manage a multicultural learning environment.

I returned to teach in Bangkok for five more years. But at some point, it got repetitive. I had done it all before. I tried to figure out what was left there for me to learn, but the situation was tapped out. I quit because one thing was missing: the opportunity to learn something new. Soon thereafter my partner and I opened the gallery and my learning accelerated.

Learning Outside of Work

If the learning in your job has reached a plateau, you could change jobs, but as I've written before, that is not the *best* answer unless you really know what you want. You also can try learning something new *outside* of work. That something could reignite your enthusiasm for your work.

My client Jeff Michaels is the country president for a luxury jeweler. He'd been in this job for seven years, but his enthusiasm for what he'd been doing had waned. For him, the time he spent getting the business started was the most exciting. Of course, the watches changed, the staff changed, his market share increased and decreased, the competition came in. But still, it was nothing he couldn't handle. He wasn't learning anything new and the challenge was gone. Now the company was running on autopilot. He had done it all, he told me. There was nothing else for him to learn.

But he didn't want to quit. He didn't want to change his lifestyle and lose out on the glamorous social life that went with his position. But he needed to do something else. I asked about his dreams, and he told me he really wanted to write. Specifically, he wanted to write a nonfiction book, but not about the luxury jewelry business.

He had a million excuses for not writing, but we talked about taking some action. He went to the Ubud Writers Festival in Bali and joined a writing group in Tokyo. He wrote early in the morning before his kids went to school, during his lunch hour, and in the evening after he was home. He found at least an hour each day for writing. And he's still writing.

His enthusiasm for his regular job has increased. He's still working on his book, but he told me it's not so important for him to get the book published. Just knowing what was missing and doing the writing has made his life much fuller, much happier—and he is no longer bored with his CEO job. The learning that has come from writing has reinvigorated his enthusiasm for his regular work.

Toward the end of my years at Keio University, I took a backpacking trip around Southeast Asia, stayed in low-price hotels and hostels, took only buses and motorbikes, and ate only the local food. I went all around Cambodia, Thailand, and Laos carrying just a knapsack. I noticed during this one-month trip that I instinctively went everywhere I could to see art and meet artists. This was not my intent when I started my journey, but it became clear that art was what I was missing in my life and what I wanted. Soon after I came back from my trip, Hitoshi and I launched our gallery.

To my surprise, running the gallery made my teaching better. As the learning about art, artists, and the gallery business accelerated, I became a better instructor in my university courses. I became much more creative in my teaching—lecturing less, playing games, hosting events in the classroom, offering new courses. I developed and taught a course on artisanry in Japanese business, which brought together my interests in art and business.

How about you? Is there something you would like to learn and do outside of work? Before you quit your job, think about something new and different you could learn that will motivate you, engage you, and be a source of even more satisfaction. Many of my clients tell me they yearn to do something more creative, and when they start painting, learning the piano, or baking cakes, their passion for work increases. Remember, when the learning stops, boredom, complacency, and cynicism all rush in to fill the void.

Learning on Your Own

The best companies provide opportunities for continuous learning. They offer in-person as well as online training programs. Yet some corporate managers tell me their training offerings are often undersubscribed. Opportunities are missed.

In North America, there are continuing education courses at universities, libraries, and community centers that provide opportunities for learning. Anyone anywhere can tap into the online resources of some of the best universities and professors via MOOCs (Massive Online Open Courses). You can listen to lectures at universities such as MIT, Berkeley, and Stanford. You can take free writing courses from UCLA online. The site for the Center for Entrepreneurial Studies at Stanford Graduate School for Business features more than a hundred videos about venture capital, business plans, entrepreneurship, and other business topics.

Create your own development plan. Write down what you want to learn and how you can go about learning it. You don't need to enroll in a formal school. There are resources for learning right where you are, as well as online and in the library. Think about adding skills that are very different from those you already have. Some companies, such as ExxonMobil, provide their leaders with alternating geographic and functional responsibilities, so a future executive learns about working in different regions as well as about different corporate functions. In this way, they prepare for global leadership roles.

Rekindle your dream and identify what you need to know to make it come true. Figure out how learning can make it happen. But beware of falling into the trap of waiting for your annual performance review to work on a development plan, one designed by your boss. Write up your own development plan. You can make your boss your partner in learning by discussing your plan with them.

One senior executive I interviewed at Publicis, the global marketing and advertising agency, had never studied business or marketing. She majored in Chinese literature and art as an undergraduate and graduate student. But once she started with Publicis, she told her bosses that learning about business was one of her priorities. She did so through dealing with clients, finding mentors, studying on her own, attending courses, and being endlessly curious.

In fact, being curious is one of the best ways to keep learning. Be like the young kid you once were who always asked "why" questions, who always wondered why things are the way they are. As I often said to my students, "Don't be so smart." Curiosity can open up so much for you. Curiosity can make any situation a learning opportunity, one that will keep you engaged. You might ask around to get the answers or you might want to research the questions even further yourself. Either way, you're acting on your curiosity.

Naïveté helps too. The singer Bobby McFerrin talks about "one of the things I have found valuable to me in a performance . . . is a certain element of naïveté," as though "as we're performing, we're still discovering the music."[2]

When I go by a McDonald's and see all the young kids in there smiling, I wonder what McDonald's does to attract them. How has McDonald's made itself a destination for families? It seems to me Burger King and Wendy's don't have the same appeal. Why? It's more than just prices. Why don't people consider healthier options for their families rather than go to a fast-food joint? This curiosity can be the catalyst for learning about the company, the food business, branding, and more.

The new drip coffee from Starbucks is called Origami, the same as the art of traditional Japanese paper folding. I am really curious how they came up with the name, if it increased sales, whether they are using the same name in every market for this product, and if I can use Japanese names in my own business. There's a lot to learn and explore everywhere.

Perhaps you wonder why your company doesn't have a certain kind of training program or offer outside educational opportunities. If that's the case, why not start a program? That's what my friend Stella Yamazaki did. Stella saw that people in her division did not know anything about using social media. She talked with her boss and put together a short training program for everyone in the division. It was because of her initiative in creating and conducting this program that she later became the assistant training director in the company's headquarters.

Remember that you can develop a particular expertise even without the seemingly necessary degree or background in that field. Jared Bernstein is best known as the former economic adviser to U.S. vice president Joe Biden, but he never earned a degree in economics. Bernstein graduated from the Manhattan School of Music with a bachelor's degree in fine arts, studying the double bass. Later, he earned a master's in social work from the Hunter College School of Social Work and a master's in philosophy and a PhD in social welfare from Columbia University. He had no degree in economics, yet he has enjoyed a successful career as an economist based on his work experience and what he learned on his own.

Too often, our work environments keep us in cubicles or towers with people who are doing similar work, but we learn the most when we interact with people who are different. We gain a point of view that may not be so apparent when we are all so similar. Strive to meet people who are different. That's one of the advantages of working in a diverse culture, with people from many places, with many backgrounds. Organizations see an increase in creativity and improved decision-making when their teams are diverse. Seek out others whose areas of expertise are different from your own.

In 1966, ten New York artists and thirty engineers from Bell Laboratories worked for more than six months on a series of performances incorporating new technology called "Nine Evenings: Theater and Engineering." Experiments in Art and Technology (E.A.T.) was founded to promote and expand these artist-engineer collaborations.

E.A.T. organized the international collaboration of more than twenty artists and fifty engineers and scientists to build the Pepsi Pavilion at Expo '70. In the United States Pavilion, works by artists together with engineers and scientists—the result of a project at the Los Angeles County Museum of Art—were shown. Robert Rauschenberg created a series of interactive works in collaboration with engineer members of E.A.T.

Break out of the box of being the finance guy or the manufacturing guru. You know more than you might think about other areas and can make significant contributions to those areas. At first you may be forced back into your box, but be persistent, insist on thinking more broadly and learning and making a contribution beyond what you and others see as your particular expertise.

I was pegged early in my career as a human resources consultant. But I got tired of it. I told my clients I could help them with marketing overseas as well, but they wouldn't hear of it. They had me branded and I couldn't change my brand. I made a shift to working on marketing with other clients, but as I think back, I wish I had been more persistent, studied more, and also showed them more of my overseas marketing expertise. I needed to market myself better.

Beware the Easy Answer

Recently, I was sitting with a focus group of finance people at a client's offices. "Why is it so difficult for us to recruit accountants?" the director of finance asked. He didn't wait for an answer. "We don't pay enough," he announced. "They don't want to work for a small company," another manager in the group volunteered.

But later that day when I conducted exit interviews with two accountants who were leaving, they complained about the lack of uniform procedures and the concern that the computer system was out of date. It was not salary or the size of the company (although the company size may have influenced them) that led to their decisions. There was much more to it. We have to go beyond the easy answer, the one that confirms our hunches, and learn what the true answer is.

I'm a fan of true crime stories and crime novels. The first detectives on the scene look for clues and make a point of keeping all their possibilities open rather than zeroing in on one suspect or one motive. Sure, a family member or friend is a likely possibility, but focusing too narrowly on them might lead the detectives to notice only clues that support that conclusion and ignore other possibilities.

"How was your trip to France?" a friend asked me. "Not so good," I told him. "I didn't enjoy Paris at all. I thought the people were rude." He jumped right in with a reason, the one that seemed most likely: "Oh yeah, they don't like Americans there." But was that really the reason? Didn't he know I was there with my Japanese partner? Maybe I was sick. Maybe I backpacked and stayed in a low-priced, less-than-comfortable hotel. There are many possible reasons why I might not have enjoyed the trip. He really didn't know. He just assumed the easy answer.

More Ways to Learn

One of my professors in graduate school told me that teaching about a field is the best way to learn about it. And when I started teaching, I discovered it was true. I needed to know what I was talking about when I taught. I had never been a leader when I taught all those courses in leadership, but after teaching about it, I did develop leadership skills. I always thought I was teaching leadership, not realizing I was becoming a leader. Writing helps too. In his book *Writing to Learn*, William Zinsser makes a strong case for his claim that writing about a field of knowledge is the best way to immerse oneself in it and to make it one's own.[3]

You can make learning part of your dream by structuring your work for learning. As a professor, I resisted lecturing and ran the classes more like a design studio than a lecture course. Each of the students' presentations and work was unique. The students gave presentations, held trade shows, and went on field trips—and we all learned.

It is common for most graduating university students in Japan to go on a trip to Europe or America. But it's the students who go to places like Kazakhstan, Rwanda, and Myanmar who learn something special and come back with experiences that really touch them. They go there not to see internationally known landmarks, but to get immersed in the culture and learn something unique.

As you create the life you want at work, one of the most important, most essential things you can learn is how and why to make work fun. We'll talk about all that fun in the next chapter.

CHAPTER NINE

Make Work Fun

When I leave home to go to work in the morning, I say, *"Itekimasu"*—"I'm going." Hitoshi sees me off at the door and tells me, *"Itte rashai"*—"Please go and come back." He adds something else too: "Have fun." He always tells me to have fun.

Although I have heard this from him so many times, I never get tired of hearing it. It makes me think about making sure my day will be fun, and it slows me down (which is a good thing). I might be going to meet a client, give a talk, or do some writing. But when he says, "Have fun" to me, it's a reminder to make work fun no matter what I plan do. No matter how difficult the situation. I promise him and myself that I will make fun a priority.

For some people, the words *work* and *fun* never seem to go together. I watch people heading to work or rushing to their offices near my home and they don't look like a happy bunch. Fun seems far from what they expect at work. But think about it. You spend so much time at work. Why not make it fun?

I tell my students, clients, and friends to make work fun. Their reaction is sometimes "What?" or "Yeah, sure, okay." But when they do make work fun, they change in ways that are remarkable. They stop complaining; they have smiles on their faces. They even seem to stand taller and move more quickly. Fun begins with something you can control: your intent. In the words of Abraham Lincoln, "Folks are usually about as happy as they make their minds up to be."[1]

Mention the idea of fun at work and people think about contests, dressing up on Halloween, telling jokes, or slamming the boss. But these have their limits. The best fun comes from surprises as well as from the work itself.

Getting Started with Fun

It's hard to break away from the notion that work has to be serious. It's almost as if there are signs in some office buildings that warn, "No fun allowed" or "All laughter will be subject to immediate disciplinary action." It's as if having fun might interfere with getting the work done. I'd be willing to bet it not only won't hurt your productivity, it'll actually increase it.

I love it when I see smiles and hear laughter in a company. I'd like to see more of it. Instead, I listen to clients talk about key performance objectives, people problems, and their toothpaste marketing campaigns with the same seriousness as a surgeon talking about a triple bypass.

You can start with something as simple as what I hear every morning. Tell people to "have fun" after you greet them. You'll be surprised at the effect. Make fun a priority for the day. You say you're under pressure to sell five thousand gallons of paint thinner? Could you make selling a game you play with clients? You could make a joke about it: "Put your paint on a diet."

If you find your boss difficult to deal with, make a game out of trying some new behaviors to see which ones work to make him ease up, maybe even smile. When he tells you he is in a bad mood, what could you say in return? Ask him what you could do to help. There is nothing like an unexpected sincere answer to turn a sour relationship into a positive one.

I recently visited an office that featured a huge Godzilla in the lobby to greet people as they came to work. I laughed when I saw it. Perhaps you heard about the huge duck that floated in Hong Kong Harbor as part of an art exhibit. Putting that same duck in an office would certainly make the environment more fun. But don't keep it there too long. A dusty, deflated Godzilla or duck soon loses its impact and becomes part of the woodwork.

Why not put some food on the table at meetings? Everyone likes to eat, and food helps people relax. I will never forget the look on the other professors' faces when a colleague brought in a cake for everyone to share. You'd think she had bought them a round-trip flight to Hawaii. They squealed like kindergarteners. There's a reason why Google gives its employees free food. It makes people feel comfortable.

Surprise enables you to have fun with others. Do things that are different from what people expect. Small things like, "I got you a coffee" get a meeting off to a good start. You might think this is not about fun, but more about generosity. But it's generosity that enables you to have fun at work. You feel good when you do something for others.

The summers in Japan are oppressive. The normal greeting in the summer months is, "Hot, isn't it?" But what if instead you said, "It's not so bad," or even, "It's cold"? You would get some strange looks, but it's likely you'd get a smile or a laugh. You become more engaged with people. You develop relationships that go beyond the greeting.

People expect comedian and actor Bill Murray to be funny. They've seen him in movies or onstage. But Murray manages to do funny things even when he's not performing because he surprises people. According to one of the many urban legends surrounding Murray's antics, as he travels around the world and sees someone eating french fries in a restaurant, he'll take one fry from their plate, dip it in their ketchup, and say, "No one is ever going to believe you." He then walks away.

He's right. No one will believe them, if in fact it did happen. Whatever the case, Murray is a guy who clearly knows how to have fun.

We can easily get into routines in our dealings with people. Try something different. In our normal interactions with customer service reps, we usually expect to hear "no" to our requests, but companies that deliver great customer service, like the Ritz-Carlton hotels, know how to surprise people. Ritz-Carlton makes guests feel welcome with a simple motto: *The answer is yes; now what was the question?* Instead of casual Fridays, try dress-up Mondays. Get the idea? Of course you do. Now try it.

Fewer Rules = More Fun

These things help, but if you want people to have even more fun on a regular basis, relax the rules. There's nothing that can ruin fun more than saying, "It's against the rules," and believing it. A big fat rule book kills fun and happiness. No matter where you are in an organization, figure out which rules to follow and which rules to ignore. Many of the CEOs I have worked with have not been strict rule followers. In fact, most of them have been consistent rule breakers. They've figured out which rules really matter and which ones don't.

When people have more freedom, work will be a whole lot more fun. You won't lose your best employees to your competitors either. Think about Southwest Airlines and Zappos, companies loved by both their employees and their customers. Southwest gives tremendous latitude to flight attendants as to what they wear and what they say. Zappos does not measure employee productivity by the amount of time they spend on the phone. The people who answer their calls are empowered to take as much time as needed to take care of the customers and make them happy. There is no script to follow.

I worked with one client who would punish people for making personal calls or checking personal email at work. He'd put a letter in their personnel file documenting this *transgression*. Talk about treating people like kids! Yet he told me he wanted his employees to have more fun at work and was looking for a creativity consultant. "Don't waste your money," I told him. How can people be their most creative when they are being constantly monitored? When there are severe controls on behavior, it's all but impossible to have fun.

Fun in the Work Itself

Shinobu Namae, the Michelin-starred chef whom I wrote about earlier, tells me that fun is an important element in everything he does. "If it stops being fun, I'll do something else," he says. The American painter Robert Henri once said, "You should paint like a man coming over the top of the hill singing."[2] Author William Zinsser says this kind of enjoyment is "a crucial ingredient in writing."[3] Your work should be the same.

When I met up with Philippe Bouvoir, he told me what I love to hear: "Work is so much fun for me." Bouvoir, a private banker from Switzerland, has worked all over the world. He had just arrived in Tokyo after a few years in Hong Kong. "What makes it fun?" I asked.

"I love solving client problems," he told me. "If they need money to pay college tuition for their son in London, I'll get it there. If they need help understanding tax laws in Germany, I'll hunt down the information they need. I can't wait to read the *Financial Times* and the *Wall Street Journal* in the morning."

Philippe is someone who has found his passion and loves the work itself. The simplest way to make work fun is to love what you do. If you're an accountant and love accounting, it will be fun for you. Ditto for teachers who love to see their students learn. I meet lawyers who tell me they love the law. Just doing the work is fun.

I wish everyone could say the same thing. No number of parties or celebrations, dress-up days or dress-down days will make the work fun if you don't like the work or the place where you do the work.

You might still think it's the time away from work that is supposed to be fun. You're supposed to live for the weekends and the holidays. But if the work itself is fun, your need for a weekend break or a holiday is much less.

Fun Personified

Do you know someone who is a mood maker? They are the people who walk into a room and everyone brightens up. They always have big smiles on their faces. They don't just *work*, they enjoy the work; they have fun with the customers and other employees.

In an earlier chapter I wrote about Hiroaki Yamane, who now works at AKQA in Portland, Oregon. Yamane always says, "Great!" when asked how he is. He's a mood maker. He faces obstacles like everyone else, but he stays strong and confident, and he doesn't let work challenges interfere with or lessen how good he feels.

Chris Moloney, who once headed the joint venture between Intercontinental Hotels and All Nippon Airways Hotels (ANA) in Japan, is another mood maker. When we first met, he greeted me with a big smile. He told me about his life, his career, his family, his dog, the wonderful time he had just had with some clients in northern Japan. We had just started working together, but it was immediately clear he is a mood maker. He enters a room and people light up. He's smiling, reaching out to people, enthusiastic in what he does. I asked him if he's always this way. He was not sure what I meant, and I soon found out there are times, of course, when he is feeling down, but he keeps those times private, sharing them only with those closest to him.

"I want work to be fun," he told me, echoing my own goal. And it is fun for him and those he works with. His job was a challenging one, integrating the global Intercontinental Hotels with the Japanese ANA hotels. But you can see him joking with hotel managers about who's going to pay for his dinner when he's making a hotel inspection. He reaches out to the young people who have just begun to work for the hotels. He enjoys being with people, and they enjoy being with him.

Maybe you know people like Hiroaki Yamane and Chris Moloney. You may not have the same personality traits as Hiroaki and Chris, but if having fun at work is what you want, you can seek them out. Fun people hang out with fun people.

And you also can become a mood maker yourself. It may not come naturally to you, but you can begin by not complaining, by seeking out people you want to be with, smiling, and not being hurled around by what happens at work. You can try to stay strong and relax. Fun really begins with freedom and confidence, which enable you to relax and be yourself at work. Being relaxed also enables you to avoid rather than participate in the dramas that sometimes occur at work. I like these three couplets from Rudyard Kipling's poem "If":

If you can keep your head when all about you
Are losing theirs and blaming it on you . . .
If neither foes nor loving friends can hurt you,
If all men count with you, but none too much . . .
Yours is the Earth and everything that's in it,
And—which is more—you'll be a Man, my son![4]

The Price of Being Too Serious and the Benefits of Fun

There are so many times when we could laugh at work, but we hold back because it looks like we're not serious about what we do. But laughing feels good and has health benefits too.

In Japan it's unusual for politicians and business leaders to show their human sides and have fun. Many maintain a "work face" that seems to be frozen in a serious expression. Those who keep their faces locked in a permanent "I'm tough" stare may scare off competitors, but they may also scare off colleagues and employees (and that might even be the intent). If you are like this, you might be disconnected from your true feelings and be isolating yourself from others. You may think you're simply maintaining a high standard, but fun need not interfere with those standards.

As Tom Stoppard writes in his play *Rosencrantz and Guildenstern Are Dead*, "Be happy—if you're not even happy, what's so good about surviving?"[5] It's hard to break people of the notion that work has to be serious. In my early days as a consultant and professor, I tried to always be serious and businesslike. But I noticed that the consultants most in demand were the ones who were different, who were not like everyone else. They were iconoclasts. And usually they were funny. The clients learned from them and enjoyed working with them. I eventually did change, not because I wanted to be like them, but because I wanted work to be fun. As I became more confident, I began to show more of myself and I had more fun.

In the bestselling book *Anatomy of an Illness*, *Saturday Review* editor Norman Cousins told how he cured himself of a debilitating illness. He had been admitted to the hospital with ankylosing spondylitis, a long-term type of arthritis that affects the spine. His condition deteriorated and his prognosis was not good. With the blessing of one of his doctors, he checked into a comfortable hotel where the food was better than the hospital and where he could watch funny movies while he medicated himself with high doses of vitamin C.[6]

Cousins got better. And he was convinced his dramatic improvement was because of his unique therapies and because he had taken charge of his own situation. Cousins is often described as "the man who laughed himself to health."[7]

Creating an Environment Where People Can Have Fun

Robert Reich, a professor of public policy at the University of California, is the star of the documentary film *Inequality for All*. At the start of the film, he introduces himself to a lecture hall full of students, telling them how he was secretary of labor under Bill Clinton. "And before that I was at Harvard. And before that I was a member of the Carter administration. And before that," says Reich with impeccable comic timing, "I was a special agent for Abraham Lincoln." He shakes his head. "Those were tough times."[8]

The students laugh, he laughs, and the atmosphere in the class becomes more fun and relaxed. Reich makes a joke about himself, and he immediately becomes more accessible and human. Robert Reich may be best known as a labor economist, but he's funny too. And although his work as a professor, researcher, and activist is serious business, he knows the importance of having fun and creating a fun environment.

When the work environment becomes more relaxed, the natural humor of people can emerge. When you reduce the distance between yourself and others by being informal, people are more likely to enjoy themselves. It's hard to have fun when you feel tense.

I made fun a priority in my classes too. Since I also had the art gallery, I had students work more on projects; I lectured less. The students explored Tokyo's business community and came back and posted their photos as if they were in a gallery. Students made presentations as if they were at a trade fair or an art exhibition opening. It was a lot more interesting and fun than the usual lectures and PowerPoint presentations.

Hillary Clinton had serious business to take care of when she was America's secretary of state, but she wasn't afraid to have fun. She got down on the dance floor in South Africa and grooved with local farmers in Malawi. Her willingness to do something different and have fun no doubt contributed to her popularity and created a positive work environment in the ultra-high-pressure world of diplomacy and foreign policy.

Another person who has added an element of fun to his work is my friend Jeff Char, whom I wrote about earlier. He's made work fun with something he loves—chocolate. Visitors to his offices often bring Jeff chocolates, which helps breaks down the barriers in their dealings with him. He posts photos on his Facebook page of the various chocolates people give him. He's kind enough to share those goodies too. It's fun, and it doesn't distract from his company's mission. People line up to sample the chocolates and talk with Jeff.

Zappos CEO Tony Hsieh recognizes that the key to his company's success is keeping his customer service representatives happy. They are on the front lines with the company's customers. He gives employees the freedom to decorate their offices as they wish. It is, after all, their home at work. He creates a culture where people are not limited to a certain number of minutes for a phone call.

Hsieh had invested in other companies, but he has frequently said he had the most fun with Zappos. Fun remains an important goal for him and the company. He recently moved its offices to Las Vegas so people could have fun twenty-four hours a day and there wouldn't be much difference between work and time off.

Hsieh once began a retreat with a unique ice-breaker. As the *New York Times*'s Timothy Pratt described the scene, "Each attendee stood up to share not-so-obvious personal anecdotes or facts, such as 'I've tried chicken-fried steak in more than thirty states.' One woman announced she had been a salsa dancing champion." Everyone whooped and hollered.

Hsieh himself demonstrated how to transmit his last name in Morse code.[9]

Zappos is now owned by Amazon, but Hsieh still runs the company, and he has kept its "zany corporate culture" strong. "This includes a workplace where everyone sits in the same open space," wrote Pratt, "and employees switch desks every few months in order to get to know each other better."[10]

Fun is really not as tough as you might think. I have heard American teens use a joke based on a combination of two clichés: "Hey, it's not rocket surgery." Even surgeons have fun on the job. Sociologist Erving Goffman studied the behavior of surgeons in the operating room. He found that many joked with the nurses and other operating staff as they performed the most serious and difficult operations. The surgeon who jokes with the nurses and staff before, during, and after an operation sends a signal that he is not just a surgeon, but is human too. Those around him can do their best work because they feel more relaxed.[11]

Goffman used the term "role distance" to refer to how people keep a separation between themselves and the jobs or positions they hold.[12] When they joke, it's a signal that they are more than the role they have assumed. Personally, they may be warm, spontaneous, and humorous, even as they are serious about what they are doing professionally. They seek to create an atmosphere where they get the job done the best they can. Perhaps if they fully embraced their roles and thought about the seriousness of what they were doing, they'd be overwhelmed and not nearly as good at what they do.

There is of course a limit to how much humor is appropriate. We want people to get the job done.

We want the people in the supermarket to get the shelves stocked. We want our dentists to take care of our teeth, our investment advisers to monitor the stock market. We don't want them to be only comedians.

Humor That Is Not Funny and a Caution

Erving Goffman also wrote about a nurse who was transferred from an experimental surgery team because her attempts at humor appeared to interfere with the work.[13] Of course, not every situation lends itself to laughter. And if someone is only funny and does not accomplish what needs to be done, he or she may not be around for very long.

Perhaps you remember a time when you thought fun at work was simply talking about the dumb things that the boss was doing or laughing at the embarrassing questions one colleague asked in a meeting. I know, I used to do those kinds of things too. But there are big problems that come with that kind of humor. After it happens, you don't feel energized. You feel exhausted. Others also suffer because of this kind of humor that makes light of a serious situation. It can quickly become ridicule.

We use this type of humor at work as a kind of armor against our own hopelessness and cynicism. It can help alleviate stress, but the benefits are short-lived. Making jokes at the expense of others may seem like fun at the time, but you usually don't feel so good afterward. It may keep us from confronting and doing something about a serious situation. Maybe we need to talk with the boss or do what we can ourselves to make the situation better instead. This kind of humor rarely makes a bad situation better, and it often makes it worse.

Once you're in the kind of work you really like, in an environment where you can laugh, you'll have the freedom to be humorous and have fun. But proceed with caution. Every workplace has someone who tells jokes. They can make the workplace fun and lighten up the atmosphere, but jokes can also fall flat. There are very few people who can tell a joke well. Sometimes when the joke is out of context, it makes everyone uncomfortable, especially when it is at the expense of someone else.

Think of fun as something that makes a situation better. You cannot force it; you can not deliberately orchestrate it. It must flow freely and naturally.

Here's an example that sounded harmless enough: A company held a "decorate your area" contest, with each employee given a nominal decorating allowance and each work group told to come up with a theme. The customer service department hung extreme sports equipment from the ceiling—reminding everyone that the company goes to extremes for its customers. The accounting department chose a pirate theme since they're always looking for buried treasure.

To me, this seems a bit forced, like doing something meant to please the boss more than simply having fun. I can't help but wonder if there was subtle manipulation by management when they came up with the contest idea. What if a work group had come up with a Hawaii display because everyone wanted to move there? Would that have been accepted by management?

Creating Community

I gave a talk at a small company recently and was surprised to find many of the people in the room didn't
know each other. They didn't know what projects the
people sitting next to them were working on. In some
cases, they didn't even know *who* was sitting next to
them. Creating a community can make work more fun
and relaxed. Connect with the people and you're creating that community.

Work gets even better when those connections are
with people who make you laugh. As I wrote before,
find the fun people and stay with them. When Bill
Clinton's advisers were asked about his relationship
with Al Gore, they answered that Gore had more
access, involvement, and influence than any previous
vice president. They added one more thing: "Al is funny
as hell."[14] There's something to be said for that trait.
Being around people who make you laugh makes work
fun. As a professor, I used to call one of the deans who
had a great sense of humor "Boss," even though that
didn't define our relationship. We'd both laugh. Perhaps
you know someone at work you can joke and connect
with in this way.

Misunderstandings and mistakes are opportunities
to laugh rather than go down the road to confusion
or anger. One time in our gallery business, we met
with an event planner from a wine company to plan a
party. We talked in round numbers about the number
of people we'd invite and the cost for wine and food.
Hitoshi couldn't quite understand the event planner's
Australian accent. She talked about inviting fifty people, serving champagne, some rosé wine, and "nibbles."

Hitoshi agreed with most of what she said, but was surprised at what we would serve. He thought she said "nipples"—not "nibbles"—and couldn't understand why they would be on the menu. We all had a good laugh. The event we planned was a success and we've gone on to hold three more events with her firm. We always have fun working with her.

When you choose people and projects, choose ones that look like they'll be fun, because of either the people or the nature of the work.

There are times when spontaneous humor works so much better than emotion. In an article in the *Harvard Business Review*, Joseph Badaracco wrote of a manager at a small regional bank who was convinced that a set of lending policies was exploitative: "When she met with her boss, she gave an emotional speech about the rights of the poor. It didn't work. Her emotionalism undermined her credibility."[15]

But humor, Badaracco writes, can make the difference. He tells about a PR manager who was upset when a partner in her law firm excluded her because of her gender from a meeting to discuss the company's affirmative action plan. She helped draft the policy. But rather than telling him how upset she was, she won points and strengthened her position when she said, "I've never been told I couldn't play ball because I didn't have the right equipment!"[16]

There are so many times when we can add humor and fun to what we do. Make them an integral part of what you want to create every day at work. In the next and final chapter, we'll talk about how the dreams you have get bigger as your life at work gets better.

CHAPTER TEN

The Dream Gets Bigger

Are the jerks gone? Are you focusing on your dreams? Are you summoning your courage? Are you having fun? Are you asking yourself every day, "What do I want to create today?" Is your life at work getting better? Are you building a great life at work?

I hope so. Congratulations on making these shifts in your thinking and in the way you work. I hope you will continue to make the changes necessary to build a great life at work. I've seen great results in working with people who follow the guidelines outlined in this book. And the most amazing result is that the dreams they once had not only come true, they become bigger.

I met up with some former clients at a reunion event we organize every year in Tokyo and was glad to hear that so many now loved their lives at work. Some had started their own companies, some worked for big banks, others were lawyers in top firms, still others were teachers and university professors. Very few had actually changed jobs. They had, however, changed the way they looked at work and changed how they worked. They were now working in a way they had never thought possible.

At the reunion, people talked about how their dreams had become bigger. One client described the joy of heading a division of one hundred people. He had once told me he'd be most happy if he could work alone. He had been trying to get through every day without getting angry. Now he told me how much he enjoyed mentoring younger workers. Another client who had been a part-time teacher at several universities had now written two books. One human resources executive who had always complained about having nothing but hassles now headed a human resources consulting company and was traveling the world. All were living their dreams and now had even bigger dreams.

They began moving in their positive, new directions by following the guidelines outlined in this book. I do not take credit for their success. I was just a catalyst for them. They did the hard work necessary. I hope the ideas in this book will also be a catalyst for you, allowing you to create the life you want at work.

It will take effort to make your new behaviors and actions a permanent part of the way you work and live. There will be days when you feel fear coming over you and you just can't seem to make anything fun. Days when even throwing your fear down the toilet in a high-rise building doesn't work. It will take some monitoring to make sure your old habits do not return and take over.

Maybe you'll resort to your old knee-jerk reaction of complaining when you get assigned a job that seems impossible. There will be days when you may have brunch with one of the jerks you thought you had let go. You'll sit there bored or angry and ask yourself, "Why did I even meet up with this person?" There will be days or weeks when you are so singularly focused on your objectives that you forget your dreams. Remember that the patterns of thinking and behavior you once had are strongly ingrained, so it's not unheard of for these old patterns to resurface when you are feeling stress or feeling lonely.

There are days when I go ahead and agree to a dinner with a former colleague I know I will not enjoy. I know he will do at least an hour of complaining. I don't cancel; I make the best of it and recognize I wasn't quite ready to get rid of all of the jerks just yet. But after I come home, I tell myself I won't do that again.

When my old patterns reappear, I try to gently put them aside. And I recognize that I still have more work to do—on myself. I recognize there is still some learning for me. Those times when I go back to my old patterns are opportunities to learn. There is always something more to learn.

When fear keeps coming back to you, it may be a good thing—a sign you are trying many new things. And when your old patterns reappear, instead of judging and criticizing yourself, recognize that habits do not change easily.

I laugh at those times now when I am not following the path I set forth in this book. I try to enjoy even those moments. I even go back and reread what I have written. Each of us learns and makes changes at our own pace. Some of our old habits are so deeply rooted and calcified that they become our first course of action, what we are most comfortable doing. But we do change. And we continue on our own unique paths.

And that's what I want to tell you as this book comes to a close. Even when you stumble or take a few steps backward in this lifelong practice, be kind to yourself. Do not get discouraged.

You are going in the right direction. Before, you didn't know what to do; now you do. There's no waiting to have the life you want at work. You have already taken steps and done the work necessary. The challenge now is to be vigilant. Things are different for you now because you know what to do, whereas before, you may have been stumped.

Your dreams will come true. And your dreams will get bigger, as they have for so many of the people I have worked with and spoken to. As I wrote at the beginning of this book, I certainly did not set out to be a role model. I just tried to figure out some things for myself so I could live a good life. But I did work hard at it and always challenged myself to grow. And my dreams came true and got bigger.

And as you do the same and go in the direction of your dreams, they too will be bigger and you too will be an inspiration to others. You will be happy with your life at work. Others will see how you work and tell you what a wonderful life you have. They will ask you, "How do you do it?"

And you can tell them it all started with the question I hope you're asking yourself every day:

What do you want to create today?

This is the question that changes lives.

References

Chapter One: How It All Started

1. "World-Class Training in ICT and Governance." GIGA Program at Keio University SFC publication, p. 2.
2. Jobbins, David. "New Ranking of Universities That Produce Global CEOs." *University World News*, September 5, 2013.

Chapter Two: It's About You (Not Them)

1. Chödrön, Pema. *The Places That Scare You.* Boston: Shambhala Publications, 2001.
2. Rotter, Julian B. *The development and applications of social learning theory: Selected papers.* Praeger, 1982, 169–235. There is also an online tool you can use to determine your locus of control: http://www.mindtools.com/pages/article/newCDV_90.htm.
3. Benson, Herbert. *The Relaxation Response.* New York: HarperCollins, 2009.
4. Jackson, Phil. *Sacred Hoops: Spiritual Lessons of a Hardwood Warrior.* New York: Hyperion, 1995, p. 47.
5. Jackson, *Sacred Hoops.* p. 48.
6. Edberg, Henrik. "Gandhi's 10 Rules for Changing the World." *Daily Good.* June 28, 2013.

Chapter Three: Dreams Have Soul; Objectives Don't

1. Thoreau, Henry David. "Conclusion." *Walden*. 1854.
2. Segren, Grace. "Dream Your Way to Success." *INSEAD Knowledge*. July 25, 2012.
3. Ordóñez, Lisa et al. "Goals Gone Wild: The Systemic Side Effects of Over-Prescribing Goal Setting." Harvard Business School Working Paper, 2009, p. 2.
4. Silverthorne, Sean. "When Goal Setting Goes Bad." *Working Knowledge*. March 2, 2009.
5. Culbert, Samuel A. "Get Rid of the Performance Review!" *Wall Street Journal*. October 20, 2008.
6. Silverthorne. "When Goal Setting Goes Bad."
7. "PISA 2006—First Results." Finnish Ministry of Education.
8. Hancock, LynNell. "Why Are Finland's Schools Successful?" *Smithsonian*. September 2011.
9. Anderson, Jenny. "From Finland, an Intriguing School Reform Model." *New York Times*. December 12, 2011.
10. Hancock. "Why Are Finland's Schools Successful?"
11. Anderson. "From Finland, an Intriguing School Reform Model."

Chapter Four: You Have to Read the Air

1. Prahalad, C. K., and Gary Hamel. "Strategic Intent." *Harvard Business Review*. July 2005.
2. Miller, Arthur. *Death of a Salesman*, act 1, scene 10.
3. Thornton, Sarah. *Seven Days in the Art World*. New York: W. W. Norton & Company, 2009.

Chapter Five: Tough Is Good

1. Yevtushenko, Yevengy. "Lies." 1952.
2. Levine, Madeline. "Raising Successful Children." *New York Times*. August 4, 2012.

3. Goss, Rob. "Great Places to Hang in Tokyo." *Time*. May 14, 2012.

4. "Domino's Pizza: Challenges Faced in Japan." IBS Center for Management Research. 2005.

5. Joe, Melinda. "A Star Turn for a Humble Ingredient." *Wall Street Journal*. June 5, 2012.

Chapter Six: Courage Matters

1. Tanikawa, Miki. "Fewer Japanese Students Studying Abroad." *New York Times*. February 20, 2011.

2. Harden, Blaine. "Once drawn to U.S. universities, more Japanese students staying home." *Washington Post*. April 11, 2010.

3. Shakespeare, William. *Hamlet*, act 1, scene 3.

4. Williamson, Marianne. *A Return to Love*. New York, HarperOne, 2012, p. 190

5. Levine, Stephen. "The Mindful Soul." In *Handbook for the Soul*, edited by Richard Carlson and Benjamin Shield. New York: Hachette Book Group, 1995.

6. Roosevelt, Eleanor. *You Learn by Living*. New York: Harper and Row, 1960, p. 41.

7. Adams, Tim. "The Interview: Robert Pirsig." *The Observer*. November 18, 2006.

8. Interview with Ida Bagus Putu Purwa. *Bali Times*. June 7, 2010.

Chapter Seven: Get Rid of the Jerks

1. Keynes, John Maynard. *The General Theory of Employment, Interest, and Money*. London, 1936.

2. Karpman, Stephen B. "Fairy Tales and Script Drama Analysis." *Transactional Analysis Bulletin*. April 1968.

3. Smith, Will. *Just the Two of Us*. New York: Scholastic Bookshelf, 2005.

Chapter Eight: Learn Forever

1. Argyris, Chris. "Teaching Smart People How to Learn." *Harvard Business Review*. May 1991.

2. Belluck, Pam. "To Tug Hearts, Music First Must Tickle the Neurons." *New York Times*. April 18, 2011.

3. Zinsser, William. *Writing to Learn*. New York: Harper & Row, 1988.

Chapter Nine: Make Work Fun

1. Marsden, Orison. *How to Get What You Want*. Thomas Y. Crowel, Company, 1917, p. 47.

2. Will, George F. "William Zinsser and Good Writing as Art." *Washington Post*. March 13, 2013.

3. Will. "William Zinsser and Good Writing as Art."

4. Kipling, Rudyard. "If." *Rewards and Fairies*. 1910.

5. Stoppard, Tom. *Rosencrantz and Guildenstern Are Dead*. Act 3.

6. Cousins, Norman. *Anatomy of an Illness: As Perceived by the Patient*. New York: W. W. Norton and Company, 2005, pp. 42–45.

7. Hagerty, Barbara Bradley. "Laughing Back to Health." *NPR Books*. May 17, 2009.

8. *Inequality for All*. dir. Jacob Kornbluth. Perf. Robert Reich. 72 Productions, 2013

9. Pratt, Timothy. "What Happens in Brooklyn Moves to Vegas." *New York Times*. October 19, 2012.

10. Pratt. "What Happens in Brooklyn Moves to Vegas."

11. Goffman, Erving. *Encounters: Two Studies in the Sociology of Interaction*. Indianapolis: Bobbs-Merrill, 1961, pp. 102–134.

12. Ibid.

13. Ibid., 114.

14. Rankin, Robert A. "VP Gore Quietly Takes On Role as the MVP in Clinton Presidency." *Seattle Times*. November 26, 1993.

15. Badaracco, Joseph L. "We Don't Need Another Hero." *Harvard Business Review*. September 2001.

16. Ibid.

Suggested Readings

Adachi, Sachiko. *To Live as We Are*. Chiba: The Angel Sachi Foundation of Chiba, 2000.

Angelou, Maya. *Wouldn't Take Nothing for My Journey Now*. New York: Random House, 1993.

Bellman, Geoffrey M. *The Consultant's Calling: Bringing Who You Are to What You Do*. San Francisco: Jossey-Bass, 1990.

Bennis, Warren G., and Joan Goldsmith. *Learning to Lead*. Cambridge, MA: Perseus Books, 1997.

Berne, Eric. *Games People Play*. New York: Grove Press, 1964.

Bohm, David. *Unfolding Meaning*. London: Routledge, 1985.

Bridges, William. *Managing Transitions: Making the Most of Change*. Reading, MA: Addison-Wesley, 1991.

Bridges, William. *Transitions: Making Sense of Life's Changes*. Reading, MA: Addison-Wesley, 1980.

Buber, Martin. *I and Thou*. New York: Charles Scribner's Sons, 1958.

Cameron, Julia. *The Artist's Way: A Spiritual Path to Higher Creativity*. New York: G. P. Putnam's Sons, 1992.

Chödrön, Pema. *The Places That Scare You*. Boston: Shambhala Publications, 2001.

Crawford, Matthew. *Shop Class as Soulcraft: An Inquiry into the Value of Work*. New York: Penguin, 2009.

Csikszentmihalyi, Mihaly. *Flow: The Psychology of Optimal Experience.* New York: Harper & Row, 1990.

Cudney, Milton, and Robert Hardy. *Self-Defeating Behaviors: Free Yourself from the Habits, Feelings, and Attitudes That Hold You Back.* New York: Harper Collins, 1991.

Fritz, Robert. *The Path of Least Resistance: Learning to Become the Creative Force in Your Own Life.* New York: Fawcett Columbine, 1984.

Fryba, Mirko. *The Practice of Happiness.* Boston: Shabhala, 1987.

Goleman, Daniel, et al. *The Creative Spirit.* New York: Penguin Group, 1992.

Heider, John. *The Tao of Leadership.* Toronto: Bantam Books, 1985.

Herman, Stanley. *The Tao at Work.* San Francisco: Jossey-Bass, 1994.

Herrigel, Eugen. *Zen in the Art of Archery.* New York: Vintage Books, 1971.

Hoff, Benjamin. *The Tao of Pooh.* New York: Penguin Group, 1982.

Jackson, Phil. *Sacred Hoops: Spiritual Lessons of a Hardwood Warrior.* New York: Hyperion, 1995.

Jampolsky, Gerald. *Love Is Letting Go of Fear.* Berkeley, CA: Celestial Arts, 1979.

Jeffers, Susan. *Feel the Fear and Do It Anyway.* New York: Fawcett Columbine, 1987.

Kabat-Zinn, Jon. *Wherever You Go There You Are: Mindfulness Meditation in Everyday Life.* New York: Hyperion, 1994.

Kahnweiler, Jennifer. *Quiet Influence: The Introvert's Guide to Making a Difference.* San Francisco: Berrett-Kohler, 2013.

Levy, Mark. *Accidental Genius.* San Francisco: Berrett-Kohler, 2010.

Livsey, Rachel. *The Courage to Teach: A Guide for Reflection and Renewal.* San Francisco: Jossey-Bass, 1999.

Macleod, Hugh. *Ignore Everybody.* New York: Penguin Group, 2009.

May, Rollo. *The Courage to Create.* New York: W. W. Norton & Company, 1975.

Miller, Alice. *The Drama of the Gifted Child.* New York: Basic Books, 1981.

Miller, Alice. *From Rage to Courage.* New York: W. W. Norton & Company, 2009.

Moon, Youngme. *Different: Escaping the Competitive Herd.* New York: Crown Business, 2010.

Moore, Thomas. *Care of the Soul: A Guide for Cultivating Depth and Sacredness in Everyday Life.* New York: HarperCollins, 1992.

Palmer, Brooks. *Clutter Busting: Letting Go of What's Holding You Back.* Novato, CA: New World Library, 2009.

Pink, Daniel. *A Whole New Mind.* New York: Riverhead Books, 2005.

Rainwater, Janette. *You're in Charge.* Marina del Rey, CA: DeVorss & Company, 1989.

Schor, Juliet. *True Wealth.* New York: Penguin Group, 2010.

Schumacher, Ernst. *Small Is Beautiful.* London: Harper & Row, 1973.

Scott, Susan. *Fierce Conversations.* New York; Berkley Publishing, 2002.

Seelig, Tina. *What I Wish I Knew When I Was 20.* New York: HarperCollins, 2009.

Stone, Douglas et al. *Difficult Conversations.* New York: Penguin Group, 1999.

Treasurer, Bill. *Courage Goes to Work.* San Francisco: Berrett-Kohler, 2008.

Tzu, Lao. *Tao Te Ching.* London: Penguin Group, 1963.

Wheatley, Margaret J. *Turning to One Another: Simple Conversations to Restore Hope to the Future.* San Francisco: Berrett-Koefler Publishers, 2002.

Whyte, David. *The Heart Aroused.* New York: Doubleday, 1994.

Zeldin, Theodore. *Conversation.* London: The Harvill Press, 1998.

Acknowledgments

I have been told that writing a book is a marathon, not a sprint. That's turned out to be very true. In my case, I could not have done it alone, without the cheering of so many people. A very big thank-you to all who have helped in forming and encouraging the ideas contained in these pages.

I'm very fortunate to have had great teachers in my life. No doubt that is why I became a teacher. The late Janet Barrows was my sixth-grade teacher, and I can still remember how she encouraged me and the entire class to learn. My thinking began to take shape at Wellesley High School, where teachers Alice Teed and Robert Lemer stand out. They taught in unique ways I will never forget. They were not afraid to show who they were. They made their classes come alive.

At the University of Massachusetts, Donald Streets, Ron Ware, Jack Wolf, Robert Dale Taylor, Parker Worthing, Dwight Allen, and Mark Rossman were the kind of professors I wanted to be.

At Boston University, Tim Hall, Leonard Zaichkowky, Gerry Fain, and George Labovitz inspired me and encouraged me to become a professor. Gerry guided me through the whole dissertation process, and I would not have been able to put *Dr.* before my name without Gerry's guidance and encouragement.

In California, it was my friend Andy Kincaid who twenty-five years ago started asking me, "Where's your book?" Here it is, Andy. A big thank-you to all the clients and companies I have worked with. In many cases, we learned together and became friends.

My longtime good friends Tom Pedersen, Roy Tomizawa, and Karen Hill Anton were the ones who pushed me to get my thoughts down on paper. Many years ago, Liane Wakabayashi taught me the importance of telling a story that connects with my own experience. I had help figuring things out in my life from Aaron Lazare, Rosalind Barnett, Lee Birk, Jim McRae, and Claudette Bouchard. Claudette has been there to cheer me on for almost twenty-five years.

I am so grateful to Keio University for giving me the opportunity to be a member of the faculty there and for putting me in contact with brilliant colleagues and students. A very big thank-you to the faculty of Business and Commerce and all the students who enrolled in my classes. You taught me as I taught you, and you enriched my life. The late Norio Tamaki encouraged my scholarship and became my good friend. Takeshi Yukawa, Takeshi Kawada, Yoshitaka Naruse, Atsushi Seike, Walter Vogl, Yoshio Higuchi, Junko Asakawa, Tomoko Yoshida, Reiko Ohya, Mathew Hanley, and David Shea were colleagues who made work a pleasure.

There would be no book if it were not for Herb Schaffner. Herb helped me organize my thoughts and develop an outline. He guided and coached me through the whole writing process, edited the manuscript, and steered me to BenBella Books, which became my publisher. I got the job done because of Herb. He was there working with me every step of the way.

I'm thankful to the entire BenBella team, including Glenn Yeffeth, Adrienne Lang, Jennifer Canzoneri, Alicia Kania, Jessika Rieck, Cameron Profitt, and Sarah Dombrowsky. All were great to work with. Not one of my questions went unanswered as the book moved from draft to finished product. My BenBella editor, Brian Nicol, edited this book as if it were his own. He brought his considerable skill and dedication to this project, and it's better as a result. My thanks also go out to our most diligent copy editor, Stacia Seaman.

Geoff Bellman, Mark Levy, and Arielle Eckstut are the ones who helped me sharpen my ideas. People ask me whom I would recommend if they are considering writing a book. The people I am thanking here are the ones I recommend.

I also want to thank the artists we work with in our art gallery. Thanks to Giang Nguyen, Jun Ogata, Mario Tauchi, Masako Kamiya, Joji Shimamoto, Hiroki Ito, Takako Sato, Ono Kouseki, Agus Bagul Purnomo, Dodit Artwawan, Ida Bagus, Putu Purwa, Zhu Wei, and Hengki Koentjoro. Shinsuke Tojima, who has been our website designer for many years, never stops touching me with his creativity and kindness. All of these artists have inspired me with their work and with the way they live their lives.

Several friends and colleagues reviewed earlier versions of specific chapters and made helpful comments. I'm indebted to Roy Tomizawa, Marc Martinez, Michael Johns, Tom Pedersen, Bumpei Sunaguchi, Charles McJilton, Karen Hill Anton, and Yuki Fukumoro for this help. Shun Ito took on the task of researching and organizing the notes and reference sections.

My sisters Fran Tobin and Pamela Burstyn provided emotional support and continuous encouragement.

All mistakes and omissions are mine and mine alone.

Finally, I'd like to thank my partner, Hitoshi Ohashi. This book is dedicated to you, Hitoshi. I would never have been able to write it if I had not met you. Not only would the book not have happened without you, but if not for you, there would be a very different Bob Tobin.

About the Author

Dr. Bob Tobin is a consultant, executive coach, and conference speaker who has consulted to organizations such as IBM, Gap, NEC, AIG, Disney, CitiGroup, the European Commission, the U.S. Navy, UBS, and Louis Vuitton. He was a host of Japan's most popular educational program on NHK and a commentator for the Boston ABC-TV affiliate.

Bob has taught at universities throughout the United States and Asia. He was the first tenured American professor at Japan's Keio University Faculty of Business and has inspired thousands of students in his courses on leadership, creativity, communication, and change. He is now professor emeritus at Keio University.

Originally from the Boston area, Bob now lives in Tokyo. He received his doctorate in human and organizational development from Boston University. He writes a blog at drbobtobin.com and co-owns and operates the Tobin Ohashi Gallery, which *Time* magazine called one of the four best places to see art in Tokyo.